BEAUTIFUL GAME

BEAUTIFUL MEMORIES

Aston Villa: My Pride and Passion

John Flanner MBE

Published by John Flanner MBE 2017

Printed by Biddles 2017

Biddles
Castle House,
East Winch Rd,
Blackborough End,
Kings Lynn,
Norfolk
PE32 1SFX

ISBN 978-0-9934175-5-9 (Paperback version)
ISBN 978-0-9934175-6-6 (Hardback version)

Typeset in Calibri 12pt by re:creates

Cover photography and design by re:creates

Printed in Great Britain.

Contents

Foreword

It's a moment I will always cherish. Cup Final day 2015 finds me in the unlikely scenario of strolling up Wembley Way with Peter McParland, reminiscing about his two goals which won the final for Aston Villa 58 years earlier.

We agree it has been far too long since the boys in claret and blue have got their hands on the famous old trophy. And while Peter is undeniably proud to remain the last player to score a Cup Final winner for Villa, he desperately wants his feat to be emulated by a current player later this afternoon. Sadly, his wish doesn't materialise. Villa's 4-0 defeat by Arsenal in the nation's showpiece game could hardly be more emphatic. But that's another story. For me, the highlight of the day will always be that pre-final chat with a true Villa legend – and it happened because of the author of this book.

John Flanner had asked McParland, one of his boyhood heroes, to join him for coffee at a nearby Starbuck's a few hours before kick-off, and the former Northern Ireland international was happy to oblige. And why wouldn't he? This man, after all, could recall watching the 1957 final against Manchester United on TV as a boy, so when John met Peter the event was reported both in the press and on television.

Having known John from my time as Villa's programme editor, I was also invited to pop along with my colleague Emily Liles from club's media department, which is how we came to be chatting with Peter on our way back to the stadium. Peter was understandably honoured to meet John Flanner, who had been awarded the MBE a few months earlier for the motivational speaking which has inspired countless people around the country. John had also written a book and was just about to publish his second. Now he is on to his third and I'm delighted to have been asked to write this foreword.

Factual books about football are plentiful, of course. I should know – I've written a few. As John readily acknowledges, though, he conducted precious little research for this one – and it's all the more enjoyable for that. Don't get me wrong, there's a fair sprinkling of factual information throughout the pages of Beautiful Game, Beautiful Memories. But essentially it is more about how John feels about football in general and about Aston Villa in particular. John's depth of feeling about his beloved Villa is arguably stronger than anyone who watches from the Holte End. He has been blind for half a century and the last match he saw with any clarity was the 1966 World Cup Final. But the loss of his sight has never robbed John of an uncanny insight into what makes a football club tick. This is a very personal story of one man's love affair with Villa, from his early days as a youngster at reserve matches to his thoughts on the modern game. He mourns the loss of football as he knew in his youth, and even makes a few radical suggestions about how the game's rulebook could be changed to improve the entertainment value for those of us lucky enough to watch matches rather than having to rely on a running commentary from a family member.

The bulk of the book, though, is devoted to John Flanner's undying support for his favourite club. As he points out; *"Not even being blind can take away the thrill and excitement of being at Villa Park on match days."*

Rob Bishop,
Football Journalist and former Programme Editor, AVFC

Prologue

Isn't it great when people get together and talk animatedly about the things they love? It can be an invigorating thing to be involved in fervent debate and heated discussions where everyone involved is free to offer their legitimate view on a particular matter.

I especially love it when sports fans in general and football fans in particular get together to discuss the issues of the day. Local pubs have flourished on this kind of debate for more than a century with passionate supporters offering pre-match views and post-match analysis. The banter is often highly charged with emotion and no less entertaining.

Wherever you go in the world it seems as if there are always people around who want to talk football. The topics covered are widespread and range from the local club to Premier rivalries, great games and players to the proverbial donkeys of the game, the best goals ever seen to the finest saves ever made, the strangest refereeing decisions to the game's quirkiest trivia. Football discussions and heated debates reign supreme, and even the surfeit of radio and television channels devoted to such has failed to quench the thirst for replaying every angle of every game.

My book of memories therefore is designed to add to and stimulate the debate even further. I want to reflect, from memory, on some of the great games, great players, great goals and maybe too some of the odder moments in my sixty years or more of following the beautiful game. I have unashamedly done little in the way of research, because when people are talking about such matters down at the pub they don't research do they? Hopefully my reflections, thoughts and opinions offered along the way will trigger some great memories for you and also offer something by way of hope for the future.

If nothing else, I trust you find the book highly entertaining and are able to use it as a means of getting your reflective juices flowing so that you too can begin to relive some of those magical moments that are tucked away in the recesses of your footballing brain. Because I have relied on memory it may be that one or two of my stories are not 100 per cent accurate, but hey, isn't that what football chat is all about?

Enjoy and get involved...

John

Introduction

Although I have passionately supported Aston Villa since 1956, I have to say that it is football as a whole that has added so very much to my life. Football has always given me such a great buzz; from a very early age I can recall having something at my feet to kick around. If it wasn't a ball of some description, then a stone would suffice.

Not being too bright academically, I often felt inferior to others but give me a football and I was happy to be one of the lads. I may not have been the best player around, but football is about dreams and I imagined myself as Peter McParland (my first Aston Villa hero about whom there will be more later). In my mind, I saw myself tearing down the left wing, cutting inside and unleashing an unstoppable shot into the top right-hand corner of the net. The fact that the pitch was a dusty old Birmingham street, the goals were a couple of factory gates, and the players if they existed, were often of negligible ability did not matter in the slightest. The dream was alive; the fire was within and having been smitten with the football bug it was destined never to die.

Now in my early seventies and more than half a century on since seeing my first live match, I have hundreds of memories of great matches, brilliant players and wonderful goals. I have experienced the joy of winning promotion, championships and cups, contrasted starkly with the despair of relegation. As I share my thoughts with you over these pages, I hope my passion for this great game will set your pulses racing as you activate your memory bank and appreciate the privilege of being part of such a wonderful game - the one we know as Association Football.

Chapter 1 - The Early Years

The first four years of my life were spent in the Aston district of Birmingham. My parents then moved to the Vauxhall area in order to take up residence in their first council house. 17 Scott Street was to be home for the next seven years and it was during those days that my love for football was to be fanned into flame.

There were a lot of children around in those days; the girls played their games in the street - dolls, prams and skipping ropes aplenty - but the boys played football from one end of the street to the other, at least we did when we were not playing Cowboys and Indians using Mum's broom as the imaginary horse. Those gravel streets and concrete paving slabs were hard taskmasters especially when you fell to the ground following a crunching tackle from behind. I still have the scars on both knees as a testimony to the fact. However, they were great days, we were all boys together sharing in our emerging love for this addictive game of ours. I recall the sound of parents, my own included, shouting down the street, "It's time to come in now," only for them to be met with the reply, "Just five more minutes". An hour later or so and in pitch darkness, an angry father or three would be pacing the street with steam rising from their heads and we knew that this was the final call. Day after day, all year round, this insatiable appetite to play football was being extravagantly indulged.

Anyway, for most of us that is as far as we got in terms of playing the game. Some of us went on to play for school teams, youth clubs and later Sunday League teams but despite great ambition, sadly we had to leave the professional side of things to those who had been blessed with a little more ability and a lot better fortune than ourselves. One of my mates David Barnes, who joined in most of our games, and with whom I walked to school every day up until the age of 11, did tell me his uncle was a professional footballer. It was only later, as my knowledge and wider interest in the game grew, that I discovered David's uncle was no less than Ken Barnes, the man who played more than 200 games as a wing half for Manchester City. Ken played a starring role in the FA Cup Final of 1956 when Manchester City beat Birmingham City 3-1 at Wembley. This was the match where the Manchester City's German-born goalkeeper Bert Trautmann played much of the game with an injury that was later diagnosed as a broken neck. What a hero, what a legend!

We only lived about a mile from St Andrews, the home of Birmingham City Football Club and that is where I first heard the magical roar of the crowd on a Saturday afternoon. Even from that distance the sound drew me and I could not wait to attend my first live game. That would have to wait a while, however, because my dad was an avid Aston Villa supporter, unlike his father, who for some strange reason was a Birmingham City fan, even though the family were from Aston. Dad often talked in glowing terms about some of the legendary players he had watched over the years. I heard time and time again of the goal-scoring exploits of the great Tom "Pongo" Waring, the lethal left boot of Eric Houghton, the canny defending of George Cummings and the battering ram of a centre forward that was Trevor Ford.

My initiation to Villa Park, as it was for a lot of youngsters at the time, was to see the reserves play in the Central League. Dad took me to see several reserve games in the mid-1950s, when I guess the average attendance would be around 4,000, and unlike today, the whole ground would be open. The size of the ground amazed me as a child, particularly the massive bank of terracing known as the Holte End. A lot of the youngsters, like myself, would get a little bored from time to time and, with the permission of our guardians would go off and play up and down the tunnels on the Holte End,

12

occasionally popping our heads up to enquire as to the latest score. One of the highlights of those reserve games for me was that Dad always bought a pork pie, which he shared with me, and a cup of Bovril, with just a little bit of salt and pepper to give it that added kick on a cold day. Boy, did I love that! The thought of it even now gets my taste buds going and you just don't seem to be able to get pork pies like that anymore!

In that era, of course, the reserve matches were always played on a Saturday afternoon at 3pm simultaneously as the first team were playing their away game. One of the exciting features of going to see the reserves was that at 15 minute intervals the score of the first team game would be put up on the scoreboards, which were situated as they are today at diagonally opposite ends of the ground. At 15, 30, 45, 60, 75 and 90 minutes all eyes would be focused off the pitch and on to the scoreboard to see how the Villa first team were getting on. It was a really tense atmosphere waiting for the score to come through, but when it did there was a huge release of emotion; the nature of that emotion was determined by the news, which came through via the scoreboard, not electronic of course, but numbers put up manually by the operators. If by some wonderful miracle the Villa had scored away on their travels, then the identity of the goal scorer would be depicted by his shirt number being displayed on the scoreboard. Believe it or not it was really gripping stuff; it was like having two games for the price of one - there we were watching the reserve match but at the same time being kept in close touch with the first team too.

The only comparable thing I can think of is that many years later when I was living in Cornwall, Dad and I had this arrangement whereby he would phone me when there was a goal. He would give two rings if the opposition had scored and four rings for an Aston Villa goal. None of my family was allowed near the phone during the course of a game and it was so tense waiting for the phone to ring. Occasionally during the course of the match the phone would ring more than four times and so we knew it was an unrelated football call and my wife, Sylvia had the task of closing out the conversation as quickly and as politely as possible!

One memorable afternoon around Christmas time, Villa were playing Manchester United. This was in the 1980s before the days of national blanket radio coverage of football. I was on washing-up duty after lunch when the phone rang not long after kick off. "Blow me", I thought "Manchester United have scored already". The phone rang four times, however, to indicate that Villa were 1-0 up. My son and I danced around the kitchen in what could have been premature celebration. Not a bit of it though because Villa went on to win 3-0 and at the end of the game I would ring Dad up for a full-time report, which he would often broadcast live down the phone from BRMB, the local commercial radio station. What emotions there were in the Flanner household in those days as we followed the Villa by phone.

As I have already said, there was no television or radio keeping you up to date with second-by-second score flashes from around the country as we have today. In the 1950s and early 1960s we just had Eamonn Andrews presenting Sports Report broadcast on the BBC Light Programme from 5-6 pm and that was your lot. No wonder why, in Birmingham at any rate, we all rushed out to the newsagents just after 6 o'clock on a Saturday evening to queue up for the Sports Argus or the Blue Mail as it was then. I know that same scenario was being played out across the country too as football mad supporters queued up insatiably for their kick by kick match reports in their local sporting pink newspapers. It is so sad that the majority of those papers have now become defunct, because there was a real charm about them.

14

On the subject of the Villa reserves I can still vividly recall some of the names of the players, indeed characters, who provided me with my early live football entertainment; Keith Jones, a Welsh goalkeeper with plenty of first team experience, and at full back we had the likes of Ray Hogg and Roy Pritchard. At centre half was a young man called Terry Morrall, who went on to give sterling service to Shrewsbury Town for a good number of years. At wing half as they were called then, were the likes of Trevor Birch, a Midlander who later moved on to Stockport County, the now legendary Ron Atkinson, who could never quite make the first eleven and a very young Vic Crowe, who later went on to captain the first team, represent and later captain Wales and also to become manager at Villa Park in the post Tommy Docherty era.

Up front we had wingers like Tommy Southren and the bald-headed Irish international Norman Lockhart. Inside forwards for some reason do not spring to mind so readily although there was Ken "K O" Roberts, a talented but very unlucky player who came to be known as being very injury-prone, and Walter Hazelden was another young starlet who never remotely realised the bright future that was predicted for him. At centre forward I recall Roy Chapman (father of the more famous Lee, who went on to make his name with Stoke City, Arsenal and Leeds United) and Billy Myerscough, the Yorkshireman who forced his way into the FA Cup winning side of 1957 following his match winning headed goal in the semi-final replay against West Bromwich Albion at St Andrews.

Down through the years there have been many other players who, though they made some first team appearances, by and large became known for their many stirring performances in the reserves. Names like Brian Handley, Gordon Lee, Wilson Briggs, Jimmy McMorran, John and Lionel Martin are the ones who immediately come to mind from that magical time in my life.

15

Chapter 2 - Catching Football Fever

My Dad started supporting Aston Villa in the 1930s, so when I was born in 1947 he could not wait for the day when he could take me along to Villa Park. I must say they are days that I look back on with great affection. Of all the memories I have of my Dad during my childhood, the ones spent with him on Saturday afternoons 'going to the Villa' are by far the most cherished, though we did also have some memorable family holidays in Blackpool.

On Friday nights before the Villa played I remember saying my prayers in bed and then including one to the good Lord saying, "Dear God, please don't let the Villa lose tomorrow". I would then have the thought, "What if the other team's fans are praying for their team too?" However, I contented myself with the notion that that was God's problem not mine and he would sort it out.

Saturday mornings would be really exciting, waiting to leave for the game. We would listen to a programme on BBC radio called Sports Parade. This was a half hour programme previewing the day's sport. They would begin with football and splitting the country up into three, North, Midlands and South, three correspondents Bill Bothwell, Dick Knight (later Larry Canning) and Clifford Webb would offer pre-match thoughts and opinions from each area. At that point it seemed as if the nation was gathered around the wireless.

That done, and making sure I had my claret and blue scarf and rattle, it was time to set off to catch the bus into Birmingham city centre. After a journey lasting no more than 15 minutes we took the short walk to join the long queues waiting for the special extra football buses that were clearly marked at the front 'Villa Park'. There was a long line of football specials (unlike today) and it was magical to see the name of our great ground on the front of the bus. When the bus was full, with about eight passengers standing, we moved off leaving room for the next busload of eager fans to get on board.

It was on that bus that I really felt the atmosphere start to pick up with a buzz of animated conversation almost exclusively relating to football matters and in particularly to the Villa match that lay ahead of us. Soon many of us were getting off the bus, and usually Dad and I did not go all the way to the ground by bus. Instead, we got off at Aston Cross and walked up Church Road. The air was full of an intoxicating and unmistakeable combined aroma that came from Ansell's Brewery and the HP Sauce factory. As we walked up the hill passing these two edifices with the crowds gathering you just knew this was Aston Villa on a match day Saturday afternoon.

The reason for our early exit from the bus was that Dad usually met up with his brother Louis at the Victoria Arms on Victoria Road before home games. Dad and Uncle Lou would have a couple of pints indoors while I stood outside with other lads with a glass of lemonade and a bag of crisps. It was all great fun but I must admit that after about 15 minutes or so I became rather impatient. The crowd was becoming denser by the minute; the sense of anticipation was heightening and I just wanted to be at the ground.

Eventually Dad returned, said goodbye to Uncle Lou (who wasn't a football fan) and we headed off together to the game. We cut through Aston Park, passing the historic and awe-inspiring Aston Hall. From the top of the hill in Aston Park you can look down over Villa Park; a magnificent and majestic sight in my eyes, made even better because from a certain point in the park you could actually see onto a small part of the pitch. Hallowed turf no less! In days past, when the ground has been bursting at the seams and the doors locked, hundreds of people have gathered on the hill in Aston Park just to get that small view of the game and to be part of the great atmosphere.

I have already described my feelings about attending reserve team games and they were fun, but these paled into insignificance compared to being at a first team game with the huge crowds. Villa Park to me was, and still is an awesome place. When I was a young boy Dad would take me to the Trinity Road side of the ground. To approach that stand from Aston Park would sometimes give me goose pimples and send a shiver down my spine. It was a magnificent edifice, a unique piece of architecture even to my young eyes, with the steps up to the seated stand, the wonderful Aston Villa crest and the clicking of the busy turnstiles on to the terraces.

Dad would usually stand near the halfway line and either sit me on one of the red crush barriers that he would stand behind or - as many fathers did - put me over the railings at the front so that I could sit with other children on the track around the edge of the pitch. How unthinkable that is today, with health and safety issues!

From that vantage point I had a sensational view of the ground. There was the Witton Lane stand and terracing opposite me with the clock situated right in the centre and the roof with its eye-catching dome-like features in the middle. To my left was the Witton End, where I was to spend many happy years later as I grew up. To my right was the amazing Holte End of the ground, the steepest bank of terracing you could ever imagine, which in those days held in excess of 25,000 people. Many years later that would become my regular pitch. For the interest of those who are not historians of Aston Villa, the Holte End is named after Sir Thomas Holte. Sir Thomas was a colourful figure, putting it very mildly, back in the first part of the 17th century. The aforementioned Aston Hall, across the road from Villa Park, was his family home. If you love your British history, then a little research into the life of this man may well prove invigorating. Personally, I think if someone were to make a movie about the man whose name is known throughout the world of football because of the Holte End, it could be a massive box office hit. The Oscar-winning actor Tom Hanks is reportedly a follower of Aston Villa and I could genuinely imagine him playing the leading role.

One of my earliest memories is a match against Sunderland who had in their side a player by the name of Charlie "Cannonball" Fleming. However, on that day Villa had their own cannonball sharpshooter. Stan Lynn (known as 'Stan the Wham') playing at right back. The ground was covered in a fair amount of snow (the match would not be played these days) and it led to a wonderful spectacle. Villa won the game 5-2 but it went down in history because our Stan scored three of the goals for Villa, two of which were penalties. Stan's trademark was to go up field very casually when Villa won a right-wing corner. Leslie Smith, our number 7, would play the ball back to Stan as he approached the penalty area and Stan would lash it into the net with unerring accuracy and power. I am amazed that teams fell for the same straightforward routine time and time again. Stan Lynn went into the record books as the only full back to score a hat-trick in a game, a record which stood for many years. The record was later equalled by Bobby Cram of West Bromwich Albion and by Steve Staunton (himself to become a Villa stalwart later) when he was playing for Liverpool.

My most treasured memory of these early years is of Villa winning the FA Cup against all the odds in May 1957 for a then record-breaking seventh time – all of the others had been in the late nineteenth or early twentieth century. The final was against Manchester United, who had already won the First Division Championship and were going for that elusive Cup and League double. Matt Busby, their manager, had put together a brilliant young team containing the now legendary 'Busby Babes'. The likes of Duncan Edwards, Eddie Colman, Roger Byrne and Tommy Taylor would be lining up at Wembley Stadium before 100,000 spectators and a world-wide television audience against my beloved Aston Villa. I was only nine years of age and I would be watching the game with my Dad on our nine-inch television screen – in black and white of course! Villa players would be wearing an unusual change strip with a shirt which was mainly sky blue in colour but with thin claret stripes down it and with white shorts. I have to say it did look rather neat.

On the day both teams showed one slight surprise in their team selection. Manchester United selected the young Bobby Charlton, rapidly gaining a reputation for his explosive shooting power and destined of course to become a legend, not just for Manchester United and England, but indeed in the world game.

As for Villa, manager Eric Houghton decided to stick with Yorkshireman Billy Myerscough at centre forward as a reward for scoring the winning goal in the semi-final replay against West Bromwich Albion a few weeks earlier. Myerscough himself had come into the team for the popular and more regular choice Derek Pace who had been injured shortly before the semi-final stage. Bloxwich-born Pace was to leave Villa shortly afterwards and carve out a brilliant career for himself at Sheffield United. On more than one occasion Pace, who was remarkably short for a centre forward, was to come back and haunt Villa with his goals against us when the two clubs met.

Anyway, back to the Final. I remember being so nervous as the two teams came out to be introduced to Her Majesty Queen Elizabeth II. When it came to the captains tossing the coin for choice of ends I can remember the photographs of Johnny Dixon the Villa skipper with his hands together and looking up to heaven as if he was praying. Well I don't know if the good Lord answered his prayers because we won against all the odds. The match was, however, shrouded in controversy because early in the match my hero, Peter McParland went charging into the United penalty area and collided with the Manchester goalkeeper Ray Wood. Both players went down injured and after a lengthy stoppage, Ray Wood was carried from the field on a stretcher – no substitutes in those days remember!

Villa's Irish winger quickly recovered, but with Wood off the field with what was later diagnosed as a fractured jaw, it was left to their Irish international defender Jackie Blanchflower to go into goal. Wood later returned to the game to play on the right wing in a reshuffled United line up, before bravely returning to play in goal for the final few minutes as United searched for an equaliser. Incredibly, however, it was Villa's Irishman who was destined to win the game for Villa with a two-goal salvo in the 68th and 73rd minutes. England centre forward Tommy Taylor got a late goal for Matt Busby's team to set up a nail-biting finale, but on the day Villa were not to be denied. In our living room with Dad (Mom had gone out shopping for the afternoon with my sister Joan and brother Paul), we jumped up and down and embraced with tears of emotion as Johnny Dixon lifted the FA Cup for Villa.

The next day the whole family went into the centre of Birmingham, where we waited in Steelhouse Lane for hours to greet the team in their open top bus as they paraded the FA Cup around the city streets. Wow! I am tingling even now at the very thought of it. Who would have thought that would have been our last appearance in an FA Cup Final until the year 2000 when we lost in an appallingly boring game 1-0 to Chelsea – a match which I attended with my son

Ian, but that's way in the future; there's a lot more to pack in between now and then.

Away from Aston Villa there were some teams playing what I can only describe as beautiful football. I think of the Burnley and Ipswich Town teams that won the old first division championship back in the 1960s and the all-conquering Tottenham Hotspur team, which won the league and cup double under the captaincy of former Villa player, Danny Blanchflower.

Four games stick in my memory in particular when it came to fuelling my appreciation of the beautiful game. In 1958 Brazil beat Sweden 5-2 in the World Cup Final held in Stockholm. The football was incredible and we saw the emergence of the great Pele as the Brazilian side ruled the world for years to come. Then in 1960 Real Madrid beat Eintracht Frankfurt 7-3 in the European Cup Final; a truly mesmerising performance in which the great Hungarian forward Ferenc Puskas scored four goals. In the summer of 1966 of course England defeated West Germany in the World Cup Final at Wembley, leading to scenes of wild celebration right across the Country. Finally, in 1967, just after I had gone blind, Celtic became the first British team to win the European Cup when, against all the odds, they defeated the mighty Inter Milan 2-1 in Lisbon, thus becoming dubbed the "Lisbon Lions". How could I not fall in love with the beautiful game when I was being treated to games of such skill and passion?

Chapter 3 - The Addiction Takes Hold

The 1959/60 football season was a key one for me and a memorable one for Aston Villa Football Club. Having been relegated to the second division at the end of the 1958/59 season, Villa commenced the new season full of optimism with Joe Mercer now installed as our new manager, replacing Eric Houghton, who had led us to the F.A. Cup triumph only two years before. Joe, a classy footballer himself, was by all accounts a likeable and easy-going man – a gentleman in every sense of the word. From this season on, I commenced a run of not missing a Villa home game for the next 15 seasons. It was a record I was very proud of, and I took in many of the away fixtures as well.

In the regular starting eleven, Villa still had five players left from the Cup-winning team of two years before. These were goalkeeper Nigel Sims, right back Stan Lynn, centre half Jimmy Dugdale, left half Pat Saward and of course my hero on the left-wing Peter McParland. John Neal had come in at left back and Vic Crowe had made the right half position his very own. In the forward line as we called it in those days we had Jimmy MacEwan on the right wing, Bobby Thomson at inside right, the marauding Gerry Hitchens at centre forward and the man who was to become a good friend of mine right up to this day, Ron Wylie at inside left.

Right from the outset this team played some exciting attacking football that took us to the top of the league. Throughout the season, the top spot was hotly contested between ourselves and Cardiff City, who themselves had some quality players, none more so than their exciting centre forward Graham Moore. There was a particularly exciting period in the month of November when, in one week spanning three games, one at home and two away, Villa spectacularly banged in 21 goals. In the two away games, we scored five goals in each match at both Bristol City and Scunthorpe United. It was the home game with Charlton Athletic, however, which will always live in my memory. We won 11-1, but the game was remarkable for a number of reasons besides the amazing scoreline.

I started to watch the match from my usual vantage point standing behind the goal at the Witton End and by half time Villa were up by 4-1. Charlton's goalkeeper Willie Duff had been injured trying to prevent Villa's sixth goal in the second half, and was replaced in goal by Stuart Leary – also a fine cricketer in those days for Kent. At half time, my mate and I decided to do what you could do then and which is absolutely unthinkable nowadays. We were able to pay sixpence in old money to transfer via the turnstiles to stand at the opposite end of the ground. As Villa have always liked to do, they had kicked into the Witton End in the first half where we had had a great view of all of our goals. Now we were going to the Holte End, but little did we know the excitement that was in store for us.

Our rampaging forwards stuck in another seven goals without reply and Charlton changed their goalkeeper one more time during the second half. The goals were scored by Gerry Hitchens (5), Peter McParland (2), Bobby Thomson (2), Jimmy MacEwan and Ron Wylie. This was particularly unusual in the sense that it was one of the very rare occasions when all five forwards got on to the scoresheet. That's how it was in those days; a team consisted of a goalkeeper, two full backs, three wing halves and five forwards. This only really began to change when Sir Alf Ramsey's 'wingless wonders' sensationally won the World Cup for England in that glorious summer of 1966, the last big game I would actually see, but more of that later. Villa finally ran out as League Division 2 Champions at the end of the 1959/60 season and were promoted back to the top flight along with Cardiff City.

It was at the start of this season that I started to purchase the *Aston Villa News and Record*, otherwise known as the match day programme. I devoured every word and particularly loved the match reports from Villa's games during the previous week. In those days, we had about six or seven teams going right through the age range. I enjoyed reading about the reserves and up-and-coming young players in the other teams, as well as reading the pen pictures of the players in the opposition team.

During the 1959/60 season, I was proud to collect the programmes from every home game. This included two friendly games, one of them was against Scottish Club Raith Rovers, as part of the deal that brought Jimmy MacEwan to Villa Park, and the other was against top Austrian side Rapid Vienna. I loved these two programmes, because they were different and special, being mainly white in appearance with some nice photos inside – all black and white then of course.

Now my love of collecting football programmes had well and truly taken off, and I began to buy two football magazines each month. First off was the very popular *Charlie Buchan Football Monthly* and then the lesser known *Soccer Star*. I must admit I became a big fan of the latter, mainly because I liked its photographic content. There was also a full page of adverts for people who wanted to swap or buy football programmes. I began reading that page avidly and I noted that one lady would advertise every week either wanting to swap or buy programmes. To this day, I can recall that her name was Ruth Arthern, she lived in Farnworth, Lancashire and she was a Bolton Wanderers supporter.

One week she was asking for an Aston Villa programme from the match against Charlton Athletic; that's right the 11-1 game. As it happened, I did have an extra copy so I sent it to her and exchanged it for a Bolton Wanderers programme. I felt a surge of excitement sending my programme off in the post and could barely contain myself waiting for my swap to come back. When my Bolton programme eventually arrived, I could not wait to open the envelope to see what it looked like and then eagerly read its contents.

Encouraged by this experience, I decided to read the swaps page in *Soccer Star* more thoroughly to see if I had any more programmes that people wanted. Very quickly I was into swapping programmes and building up my own collection to the point where I thought it would be a great idea to collect as many programmes from other clubs that I could. I went through all of the four divisions in England and then on to the Scottish clubs. I never did lose the excitement of reading the programmes, sending out programmes to other people and then waiting for the postman to return with my swap.

Football programmes today are wonderful publications with glossy pages and fantastic colour photographs, but to my mind they lack the individuality and character of those bygone days. The programmes then were all different designs, shapes and sizes. I recall the Tottenham Hotspur programme from the late 1950s as being just a couple of foolscap (as it was before A4 size) sheets stapled together. It struck me as very poor from a top club, but at least it was different. I remember lowly Walsall came out with a great little programme. It was small, but like a book with a bright red cover. Very novel at the time and it fitted nicely into a jacket pocket without having to be folded − I hated getting creases in the programme and I do to this day. It was a wonderful hobby and it was only after many years of being blind that I decided to sell some off and give others away.

When writing this book, I found myself wondering what happened to Ruth Arthern, and after 51 years we have been reconnected over our love of the beautiful game. Ruth Crawshaw, as she is now known, is as passionate as ever about her beloved Bolton Wanderers and hasn't missed a single match since her very first game in 1957. Ruth was recently the proud recipient of the George Warburton Award for Outstanding Service in 2014, in recognition of her remarkable service and dedication to the club.

In the early 1960s Joe Mercer began to introduce a crop of young home grown players, who later became known affectionately as 'Mercer's Minors'. Micky Wright came in at right back, Charlie Aitken at left back, Mike Tindall at right half, John Sleeuwenhoek was the centre half and Alan Deakin (who eventually became captain) was at left half. By way of back up there was always right back Keith Bradley and young centre half Lew Chatterley. All of these players excelled and Charlie Aitken went on to be the player to hold the all-time record for Aston Villa appearances. I had the pleasure of seeing a home game against Sheffield Wednesday, which stands out because it was Charlie Aitken's league debut and FA Cup-winning captain Johnny Dixon's final appearance. Dixon broke his nose when scoring his goal that day, a repeat of the injury he had sustained in his very first senior match for Villa 15 years previously. He rightfully received a standing ovation on returning to the centre circle for the restart, and for the record Villa won 4-1.

Gerry Hitchens, who we had purchased from Cardiff City, was a prolific goal scorer for us and he became a massive favourite with the Villa fans. His high-kicking running style and shock of very blonde hair meant that he was easily recognisable out on the field.

In 1960/61, our first season back in the top flight, Gerry was to continue to be an outstanding goal scorer and this led to him being selected to play for England against Mexico. The game was played at Wembley and was a midweek afternoon kick off. I managed to

29

persuade my Mom to let me have the afternoon off school so that I could watch the game and as far as I know, Dad never did find out – which was a good job, otherwise we would have both been in trouble. I felt so proud as the teams came out on to the field to see my local hero Gerry Hitchens in that team and going on to lead the attack. England won the game 5-0 and Gerry marked his international debut with an exceptional goal - so it made my day.

At that time, there had been about three or four English players go abroad to ply their trade, mainly to Italy. That is where the big salaries were to be had. John Charles, Joe Baker, Jimmy Greaves and Denis Law are the few names who spring to mind, the latter two transferring for the then outstanding amount of £100,000 each. It was no surprise, therefore, when at the end of that season Inter Milan came calling and signed Gerry Hitchens for the equally impressive price of £85,000. I recall seeing a photograph of Gerry in his Inter Milan shirt and although I felt sorry that he had gone, I nevertheless wished him well and from then on, I followed his career with great interest. Suffice to say he was one of the English players who succeeded in Italy when many others have failed. The Italians really took Gerry Hitchens to their hearts and I know he was loved as a player and as a man everywhere he went. Of course, I soon learned that no matter how great a player becomes, he is never bigger than the club itself. The club and its loyal supporters remain long after the players have moved on. Gerry Hitchens had gone, but it was now time for a new personality to burst on to the scene and I mean that in every sense of the word.

I was 14 years of age by this time and I had a paper round. In fact, I really loved this job. Morning, evenings and weekends I delivered my papers for Mr Eyre, the newsagent on College Road, Erdington. My first round was called Hillcrest, but I soon transferred to the Wyrley Birch Estate round, which covered the area where I lived with my family. The round consisted of delivering to blocks of flats, maisonettes and houses. I loved it as I always imagined people being delighted when their newspaper was popped through their letterbox. Even to this day I really enjoy bringing good news and that's one of the things that motivates me to enjoy life. I always made sure the papers were put right through also, not leaving them half hanging out, getting wet in bad weather and giving tell-tale signs to would-be burglars.

I have to confess, however, that I read the back page of every newspaper as I was walking along. It was on one such Saturday morning that I can remember one of the back-page headlines in the Daily Express. It read 'Doog Signs for Villa'. The story was that Derek Dougan, who had been on the losing side in the FA Cup Final only a year or so before, had indeed signed for Villa for £15,000 as a replacement for Gerry Hitchens. Even at my tender age the thought passed through my mind that we sell Hitchens for £85,000, yet replace him with a player costing £15,000. Some Villa fans of recent times might be thinking that times never change at Villa Park.

The Daily Express report revealed that Dougan, a Northern Ireland international, had recently shaved all his hair off in protest at being jilted by his fiancé. When Dougan had his hair prior to coming to Villa and later on in his career I always thought he bore some resemblance to Jess Conrad, the rock 'n' roll singer who later came to the attention of a wider audience when playing Joseph in the Amazing Technicolor Dream coat. Anyway, Dougan soon became a fans' favourite with his incredible ball skills, heading ability and somewhat eccentric approach to life. Again, I recall him scoring a couple in a high-scoring game at Villa Park when Villa beat Leicester City 8-3.

In the big freeze of 1962/63, when hardly a game was played for two months or more, Villa played the first leg of a League Cup semi-final at Sunderland on a very cold, snowy afternoon. They won 3-1 and went on to the final with a goalless draw in the second leg, which wasn't played until April. But the thing that stands out in my memory was that as the teams came out for the second half with *'Let's Twist Again'* by Chubby Checker played over the public address, the radio commentator on what must have then been the BBC Light Programme (as we had no BBC Five Live) began to laugh because he saw Dougan doing the Twist on the centre circle as he waited for the second half to kick off! Later, after leaving Villa and having a spell in the lower league with Peterborough United, Derek went on to have a glittering career with Wolverhampton Wanderers where he formed a lethal striking partnership with John Richards.

Having discussed two of our finest centre forwards during my time of watching Villa this would be a good time to continue this theme. Traditionally number 9 is the shirt worn by centre forwards and it is the position that historically has grabbed most of the headlines. Legendary names like Dixie Dean, Tommy Lawton and Brian Clough all wore the number 9 shirts for their respective clubs and as I said earlier, my Dad always talked about the likes of Pongo Waring and Trevor Ford for Villa, both proud wearers of the number 9 claret and blue shirt.

One of my all-time favourite players followed Derek Dougan into the club and made the number 9 shirt his own for three seasons in which he scored more than 80 goals, mostly with his terrific heading ability. Tony Hateley, like Ron Wylie before him, was signed from Notts County. Tony was big and strong, fearless like all of the great centre forwards. He was lethal in the penalty box and from crosses he would come charging into the goalmouth and head the ball with tremendous power and accuracy, often giving goalkeepers no chance of preventing the goal.

One Saturday afternoon I was with my friends at a local park having a kick around. My transistor radio was propped up against one of the goalposts. Villa were playing at Tottenham Hotspur that afternoon and I wanted to hear the scores on Sports Report. The time came around to 5 o'clock and the all too familiar sound of the Sports Report theme tune began to ring out, followed by the sports headlines. They began with the familiar voice of Eamonn Andrews saying, "Spurs and Villa share a ten-goal thriller". I could hardly believe it; the score was Tottenham Hotspur 5 Aston Villa 5. At one time during the game Spurs had led 5-1, but Villa, led by Tony Hateley who scored four goals, came roaring back and could even have won the game in the last minute had not young left half Alan Deakin missed a sitter. The headline in the local Sunday Mercury next day cleverly had the headline "It's White Hot Lane for Villa".

Just like Hitchens before him, Tony Hateley's scoring exploits with Villa were so impressive that it was no surprise when the big boys came calling. In those days of the trendy, swinging sixties, Tommy Docherty and his brilliant young Chelsea side were entertaining the whole nation with their flamboyant style of football. They also had the irrepressible Jimmy Greaves in their side. Hateley went on to play for a batch of other clubs including Liverpool, Coventry City and Birmingham City.

Since then I have enjoyed following a host of brilliant number nines including Andy Gray, not the tallest of centre forwards, but certainly the most courageous. Andy was part of the Villa side in December 1976 which trounced champions Liverpool 5-1 at Villa Park on a memorable floodlit Wednesday night. In fact, all of the scoring came in the first half and Gray contributed two of the goals in one of the finest performances I have ever witnessed from an Aston Villa side. The other goals were shared between John Deehan and Brian Little, two other Villa legends.

Gray's departure was followed by the arrival of Peter Withe. This was generally recognised as a master signing by manager Ron Saunders. The signing of Peter Withe was, as it turned out, the final piece in the jigsaw of a Villa team that went on to lift the First Division Championship for the first time in 70 years, plus the European Cup and the European Super Cup. Again, as with his predecessors, Withe's performances for Villa were so outstanding that international recognition with England eventually came his way. Of course, the crowning moment of Peter's career was when he notched the winning goal (off his shin) from Tony Morley's cross in the European Cup Final against Bayern Munich in Rotterdam in May 1982.

Many other centre forwards have worn the claret and blue shirt during these years of course, but many of them hardly get a mention in the books that have been written about the club. John Woodward came to Villa from Stoke City in the 1960s but sadly got injured after displaying extraordinary talent in the preceding match against the then mighty Leeds United, scoring two of the three goals giving Villa a 3-0 victory. Sadly, Woodward hardly ever figured again.

Brian Greenhalgh came from Preston North End with his club colleague and Welsh International Brian Godfrey – they were known as 'The Bee Gees', after my favourite pop group of the same name. Godfrey went on to be a star for Villa, captaining them at the League Cup Final against Tottenham in 1971. Greenhalgh, however, though showing a lot of promise to begin with, disappeared into obscurity. Dave Simmons came from Arsenal and Sammy Morgan (another

Irish International) also came, but neither made the big impact of some of their former colleagues.

Simon Stainrod arrived from Queens Park Rangers and started with a bang. He made his debut at Exeter in a League Cup game which Villa won 8-1, with Stainrod netting on four occasions. Although he played a few other good games, niggling injuries meant that Simon never really got his Villa career going and he drifted out of the club after a year or so. Alan McInally's stay with Villa was short, but it was also explosive and spectacular. Signed from Celtic by Graham Taylor, Rambo, as he was nicknamed, soon became a big hit with the Villa fans. He scored some spectacular goals in a season which saw Villa promoted back to the First Division in 1987-88. McInally scored many fine goals that season, but his form was so brilliant that he went to Bayern Munich for a fee of £1.1m in the summer of 1989. The likes of Andy Lochhead, Tony Cascerino, Ian Ormondroyd, Dean Saunders, Dwight Yorke, Savo Milosevic and Dion Dublin have all worn the shirt over the years, but it would be true to say, we are still looking for the likes of goal-scoring heroes of old to proudly adorn the claret and blue number nine shirt once again.

Chapter 4 - Tragedy Strikes the Beautiful Game

In the early days, when Dad was mainly taking me to reserve games, Villa had a brilliant young goalkeeper by the name of Arthur Sabin, who was reportedly destined for great things. Dad and I had watched Arthur play in the reserves on a number of occasions and Arthur had always impressed with his shot-stopping ability and great agility. Arthur also impressed in the handful of first team games he got to play in place of the ever-reliable Nigel Sims.

One day when I was walking home from school, however, I was horrified to read the headlines on a newspaper stand saying 'Villa's Young Keeper Dies'. Arthur was struck down with a mystery illness just after Christmas, and taken into hospital on January 14th for observation. His condition was more serious than first thought and it transpired Arthur was suffering from kidney disease. Two specialists were called in, but still he failed to respond to any of the treatments. Sadly, on March 5th, 1958, young Arthur died in Birmingham's Queen Elizabeth Hospital. He was just 19. At his funeral, some of the Villa players who had graced the Wembley turf just 10 months earlier carried his coffin to church. Hundreds of fans turned out to pay their respects.

Paying tribute in the Birmingham Dispatch, sports writer Dennis Shaw said Sabin, *"bore the stamp of a future England goalkeeper. The loss to Aston Villa is tremendous"*.

Manager Eric Houghton remarked: *"We have lost a fine young goalkeeper, a very good prospect. We are all depressed."*

In the same year, 1958, another tragedy was to hit the world of football and this time the story would not be confined to Birmingham, but would indeed reverberate around the world. A plane carrying Manchester United players back from a European Cup tie had crashed on the runway in Munich killing a number of players, officials and journalists. Among the players to die were the legendary Duncan Edwards, Tommy Taylor, David Pegg, Roger Byrne and Eddie Colman. These were players who had not only played against Aston Villa in the 1957 Cup Final, but who I had also seen close up only a short while before the disaster. I witnessed Manchester United draw 3-3 in a pulsating encounter against Birmingham City at St Andrews. I was standing right at the front of the terraces on the half way line and to this day I can vividly see in my mind's eye David Pegg taking a throw in just a few yards in front of me.

When I began to get news of the accident on my way home from school that afternoon in 1958 I just could not take it in. These wonderful football players, so young and so brilliant, who I had seen just a few weeks before had now been caught up in this terrible accident and many of them had lost their lives. For weeks, we listened to the television and radio broadcasts as manager Matt Busby clung to life in a German hospital. After a long battle, the gravel-voiced and likeable Scotsman pulled through to the relief of everyone. Then incredibly, with Mr Busby still in hospital the new Manchester United team, made up of reserve players and emergency signings, made their way through to the FA Cup Final for the second year running. They lined up against Bolton Wanderers and with the support of the whole nation behind them (apart from those people from Bolton of course) they put up a great fight before going down 2-0 as England centre forward Nat Lofthouse grabbed both goals.

That year in fact was historic for one former Aston Villa player. Stan Crowther had played in the final for Villa the previous year against Manchester United and had started for Villa in the FA Cup the following season. Vic Crowe had now taken Stan's place in the Villa team so when Manchester United came calling Villa agreed to let Stan go to United. Stan was then given special dispensation by the Football Association to play for Manchester United in the FA Cup. This goes against their rules because no player is allowed to play for more than one club in the FA Cup in the same season. That record still belongs to Stan Crowther, he is the only man to have played in the FA Cup for one club after being cup-tied with another.

Football in the UK went by relatively unscathed after that for many years though the 1970s brought the unwelcome scourge of hooliganism. Innocent football chanting and booing gradually gave way to more sinister, abusive and obscene chanting. The first football song/chant that I began to feel uncomfortable with was one in which the Villa supporters sang, "We hate Nottingham Forest, we hate Birmingham too. We hate West Bromwich Albion, but Villa we love you". I remember thinking to myself where does hate come into this? Besides which I did not hate any of those teams. This after all was a sport and one which I loved.

Slowly but surely the segregation of rival fans began to become more evident. I actually deplore this development to this very day. With the mass segregation of opposing fans allied to the arrival of the replica shirts it is now as if we have two warring factions each wearing their distinctive uniform. It now gives me very little pleasure to sit in a ground and to witness two sets of fans baiting one another in such a hostile manner. I loved the days when I went to Villa Park with my friends with the dual purpose of seeing our team and cheering them (almost as an extra man) on to a victory. I was there to passionately support my team, whilst respecting the opposition and their travelling fans. I would totally get behind the Villa players and so did most people around me. I could not and cannot go along with this idea of "Stand up if you hate Man U" or singing songs that insult my local rivals Birmingham City or their manager. In fact, I would ask the question; How does singing such songs actually support your team?

In fact, as alluded to earlier, I used to go to St Andrews along with some of my mates who were Blues fans – although only if Villa were playing away or not playing at all. I learned to appreciate football and sportsmanship from whichever direction it came. I also enjoyed games at The Hawthorns, home of West Bromwich Albion and Molineux, home of Wolverhampton Wanderers. In attending such games, I could appreciate the skills of players in those teams and the likes of Ronnie Allen and Bobby Hope for the Albion, and Ron Flowers and Ted Farmer for the Wolves.

I particularly looked forward to the spine-tingling games between Aston Villa and Birmingham City. The brilliant thing was that pre-segregation I would stand alongside my friends who were Birmingham City supporters. It was great fun as all around the ground we would try to outshout one another with the alternative Birmingham/Villa chants. It was all about fun, excitement and enjoying the beautiful game together. I do not recall any hatred being present in those days.

Likewise, when I went to away games at the likes of Arsenal or Chelsea, Manchester City or Leeds United, it was a case of nipping into the local pub near to the ground beforehand and having a drink and a sandwich with the opposing fans. We chatted animatedly about the game we loved so much and compared players on our respective sides. We would then often walk to the ground together and invariably stand together also. On more than one occasion at the end of the match, regardless of the result, we would shake hands, swap names and addresses and arrange to meet up when the return fixture came around.

In those halcyon days of the 1960s, football was still a sport and a means of great social interaction. The segregation of fans, however, I believe changed that for ever and as one philosopher said, "If we start treating people like animals, then don't be surprised if eventually, they start behaving like animals". Throughout society wherever we treat symptoms rather than the cause of the problems then we only mask the real issues.

It grieves me that millions have lost their lives in two World Wars in the last century, fighting for our freedom, but now people are not free to go to a football match and sit where they wish with the people they wish to sit by. My grandson Oliver cannot come to a match with me because he supports Manchester United and he is afraid that if he stands up and cheers then he will be evicted from the ground. That cannot be right, it is abhorrent and I truly wonder if those war heroes were alive to see our country today, would they feel it was all worthwhile. Dare I dream that one day, football fans of whatever persuasion could sit or stand alongside each other at a football stadium in a civilised and dignified way, as they do in other sports like rugby and cricket?

The late 1970s and 1980s saw English clubs dominate in Europe, winning the prestigious European Cup year after year. Why, even my own beloved Aston Villa got in on the act winning Europe's major footballing prize in 1982, when defeating the much-fancied Bayern Munich by that one Peter Withe goal-to-nil. In 1985, however, Liverpool were contesting the final against Italian giants Juventus. No one really remembers too much about the game, but what they do remember is that 39 Juventus fans lost their lives and many more were seriously injured when a few Liverpool fans charged an area containing Juventus fans. A wall collapsed under the pressure and carnage resulted. I remember listening to the commentary on BBC Radio 5 and as I listened to that doyen of all radio commentators

Peter Jones and his summariser Emlyn Hughes, the tears were streaming down my face as I listened to them describing the scenes of carnage before them.

Because of the hooligan element in our country, which had attached itself like a cancer to our beautiful game, English clubs were banned from competing in European competitions for what turned out to be five years and this, clearly slowed down the development of our younger players. This tragedy incredibly came only a couple of weeks after a fire in one of the stands at a match between Bradford City and Lincoln City had resulted in the loss of 56 lives. This certainly was a black decade for our national game and before it was through there was unimaginably, worse to come.

On the Saturday of 15th April 1989 at the Hillsborough stadium in Sheffield, Nottingham Forest were playing in one of the FA Cup semi-finals, against of all teams, Liverpool. Shortly after kick off with crowds of people still surging through the turnstiles, many people somehow got caught up in the crush. As the game continued for a short while no one had any idea of the horror that was unfolding on the terraces, but in actual fact, 96 Liverpool supporters lost their lives on that fateful day. What a cruel twist of irony that Liverpool and its supporters should be involved yet again.

Much has already been written about this so I won't say more here, except to mention that at least one good thing came out of this disaster. The government of the day ordered Lord Taylor to put together a report into improving safety at sports grounds and the very lengthy enquiry and detailed report when it came out, ordered that all top-flight football grounds in the Football League should become all-seater stadiums, which duly took place. Many of us devoted fans have bemoaned the loss of our terraces – we maintain that football is a game of passion and it is very hard to sit down to watch a game, unless it is incredibly boring that is! I cannot deny, however, that since all seater stadiums have become the norm that not only have there been no further disasters, thank God, but also it is far easier for the police and other security bodies to maintain order at these venues.

Before leaving this theme of tragedy within football and moving on to more joyful aspects of the game, please allow me to let you in on what at the time was a pretty tragic and life-changing experience in my own life. Having come to terms with the realisation that I was not good enough to become a professional footballer, I did still of course, love playing the game. After leaving school some mates and I who lived in and around the Wyrley Birch Housing Estate in the Erdington area of Birmingham formed a team and successfully applied to play in the Sunday Alliance. To begin with we were called Parkside, so named because quite a few of the lads lived alongside Witton Lakes Park. We later changed our name to Wyrley Villa due to the fact that a man came along to coach us by the name of George Lunn. George, a tall, slim man in his sixties, had been on Aston Villa's books in the late 1930s and made a few appearances during the course of World War II.

It was while playing for Wyrley Villa that two worrying incidents are etched into my mind. Firstly, a pre-match kick about; along with the rest of the team I was drenched to the skin by a cloudburst of some of the heaviest rain I have seen in my life. Within minutes, however, the clouds rolled away and the sun began to shine. In my case, however, the rain was still dripping off my hair and into my eyes. As much as I tried to dry my eyes the water seemed to pour down into them incessantly. The game kicked off, but I was having trouble seeing clearly. Everything was blurred even though I tried wiping my eyes to get clear vision. The problem lasted until well into the game and eventually righted itself, but it was stressful for that short period of time.

A little while later, maybe a week or two, I was playing another game, this time at Senneleys Park in Birmingham. I was standing by a goalpost as I was playing at left back and defending a corner. The ball came in and seemed to be heading right for me so I jumped to try and head the ball away. I was knocked slightly off balance by an opponent competing for the ball and banged my head against the goalpost. I remember being slightly dazed, but responding to the call of the manager to get up field, I recovered my composure quickly and began to join in our attack.

Very quickly, I realised again that something was wrong and as the ball came towards me I miskicked it with my left foot. Things were just not clear. As I looked around me the other players, the goal, the ball and the views in the distance were all fuzzy. It was worrying and after running to the touchline to speak to the manager, he pulled me off the field for a while. By half time, however, I was feeling (and seeing) a whole lot better so I played the second half and then went home feeling completely fine. All was now well, or at least that is what I thought.

About two weeks or so later, I was at the office where I worked in motor cycle tyre sales at Fort Dunlop, part of the prestigious Dunlop Rubber Co. I was checking a balance sheet, but the figures were not at all clear. I went to Pam, the typist and asked her to run me off another copy as that one was unclear. Pam looked up at me and said, "John, are you serious?"

I said I was as the figures were obviously blurred. I will never forget her reply as she said, "John, they are as clear as crystal".

In that instant, the proverbial penny dropped and my mind went back to the two football incidents. I tried shaking my head and rubbing my eyes, but to no effect.

Within the hour, I was at Birmingham Eye Hospital for tests and they confirmed that I had a serious loss of sight. I answered many questions from the respective doctors and in the end, they asked me to go back the following week, stating that in light of the bang to my head, I may be suffering from delayed concussion. I duly went back the following week and the week after that and every week for up to six months and every time my sight was getting worse until eventually I was almost totally blind. Through all of my visits, however, I never imagined the day would come when I would be told the news that I would never see again. Up until then it had been an adventure, having time off work to go to the hospital. I always thought they would give me a pill, an injection or a slight operation that would solve the problem. Then as I stood with my Dad in the eye clinic on 4th January 1967 I heard the chilling words from the Consultant, Mr Vernon-Smith, "I am really sorry John, there is nothing we can do. You will need to be registered blind". It was a surreal moment and, after filling out a few forms, Dad and I left the hospital both feeling absolutely stunned.

Before getting the bus back home to break the news to Mum we stopped off at a coffee bar in the centre of Birmingham. I sat at a table while Dad joined the queue for coffee. The radio was on in the background and as I stared into space the news headlines came on. I was immediately gripped by the tragic news that Donald Campbell had been killed at Lake Coniston during his attempt on the world water speed record in Bluebird. I could hardly believe my ears as Campbell was a national hero at the time and most of us took a keen interest in his daring exploits. Tears began to fall down my face at this very sad news and as Dad came back with the coffee, on seeing me so upset, he tried to comfort me by saying "Don't worry son, we'll get through it". I tried to explain to Dad that I was not so much upset about me, but the distressing news about Donald Campbell. For Dad, however, the greater grief was that his oldest son had just been condemned to a life of blindness.

If you should want to know in more detail how I managed as a blind person, some of the fears that came into my life and how I overcame them along with some of my most embarrassing moments and funny stories then you can do so in my first book *Fear, Fun & Faith*.

Now, however, I want to concentrate again on the game I love so much. The first professional game I can recall where I was aware something was wrong with my sight was when I travelled with a friend to see Villa play Stoke City at the Victoria Ground. We stood as near to the halfway line as we could get, but even from there it was as if a mist had descended on to the pitch and it got worse as the game wore on. Certainly, as far as the Villa defenders were concerned there must have been a mist or something else in their eyes, because Villa lost the game 5-0, with former Villa hero Harry Burrows notching a superb hat-trick.

I was so fed up after the game, not just because of the result, though that was bad enough, but that I could just about make out half of the pitch. In my own mind, therefore, I decided that this would be the last game I would attend. Not long afterwards, Villa were at home to Tottenham and my family could not believe it when I said I was not going to the match. I became more and more fidgety after 2pm and at around 2.30pm one of my friends, Brian, who had in fact moved to Cornwall, knocked on my door. I was shocked to see him as I did not know he was back in the area. "Hi John," he said, "I just called on the off chance that you had not already left to go to the Villa and wondered if I could come along with you."

Brian had no idea that I was almost blind. We had played together in the same team at school and later for Parkside in the Sunday alliance, before Brian had moved to live in St Austell after marrying Lyn following a whirlwind holiday romance. In a few short minutes, Brian caught up with my news, but even in the midst of receiving this shocking news about his friend, Brian was still able to jolly me along and encourage me to go to the game with him. He said he would give me a commentary and I would still enjoy the atmosphere. I was not convinced, but I went along all the same.

We arrived at Villa Park about 15 minutes after kick off and took our place behind the goal on the Witton End terraces. Villa were already a goal behind, but it turned out to be a very exciting game which Villa came back to draw 3-3. I recall that Mike England was outstanding for Tottenham – a colossus at the heart of their defence. I thoroughly enjoyed Brian's commentary and the atmosphere too was pretty special in this dingdong encounter. Thanks to Brian I had kept up my record of not missing a home game for so many years and suddenly I had realised that not even being blind could take away the thrill and excitement of being at Villa Park on match days.

Chapter 5 - Silver Lining

Going blind at any age would obviously be a real shock to the system, but at the age of 19 with my entire adult life ahead of me it was terribly traumatic, and had it not been for the loving support of family and friends, I might have slumped into a deep and depressing world of introspection. The fact that I did not do that is a tribute to the love I received and on the near horizon were some unexpected and most welcome heroes.

One of my friends at the time, Graham, very similar in looks to the Milky Bar Kid or Joe 90 (if you can remember either of those) insisted that we should still go out to discos just as we had been doing for a couple of years before my sight loss. I must confess I was not much of a one for dancing but you had to show willing if you wanted to meet a pretty girl or two. I protested to Graham that it would be embarrassing walking into a disco with me carrying a white stick and then having to feel my way on to the dance floor. Ever the extrovert, though, Graham, who was a member of a local amateur dramatics group, was really up for it. He loved it when, with me on his arm, folk would move out of the way for us to pass by. I think it made him feel important. He honestly thought it was a right good laugh and I think his light-hearted approach to things really worked as an excellent therapy for me.

Anyway, on very rare occasions we would pluck up the courage and ask a couple of girls for a dance. It just goes to show that you never know who is watching, because during one such evening at the Heartbeat Club above the Silver Blades Ice Rink in Birmingham, a guy came up to chat with Graham and I while we were having a drink. He said that he was a junior reporter with the *Birmingham Mail* and that he had noticed me dancing (or should that be trying to dance?) week after week. He found it totally fascinating that I, as a blind

49

person, should be even attempting such a thing. He asked me for a few details about my life and said that with my permission he would talk with his editor about possibly running a story on me. Of course, I readily agreed as the thought of a little bit of fame did at the time seem quite appealing. As you might imagine, Graham was not averse to a bit of that either!

A few days later the reporter came to visit me at home along with a photographer. After answering loads of questions and posing for a photograph, the two men left and said the story would be in the paper the following day. I was so excited and couldn't wait to read what they had written. The paper duly came out and my family, that is Mum and Dad, brother and two sisters, could not wait to read the article to me. I can't remember what page it was on, but the headline of the story read "Football and Dancing for the Fan Who Can't See" and the contents of the story were totally accurate and well written – apart from the comments about me loving dancing, that is! I have to admit to being pretty proud of that newspaper coverage and it was good to receive feedback from wider family members, friends and neighbours. I was even stopped in the street by people who had read the article and for a short time I felt like a bit of a celebrity. The best was yet to be, however.

Within a few weeks of being registered blind, I was introduced to a lady who would become my Social Worker, a Devonian lass with long blonde hair (so I was told) by the name of Mary Hulme. Mary taught me mobility skills such as how to get around the streets using a white stick and depending on my other senses to pick up little clues as to where I was. Mary also introduced me to the basics of reading and writing braille. It soon became apparent I would need to buy a typewriter (manual in those days of course) and a Perkins braille writing machine.

The combined total of those would be well in excess of what we as a family could afford at the time so the football team I played for, Wyrley Villa, arranged a charity game to raise funds for me. It was to be held at the Boldmere St Michaels ground in Sutton Coldfield and would be against none other than the Aston Villa Old Stars. When the day of the game came around I got to kick off the match and then disappear quickly from the pitch. It was a joyous day when I got to meet a number of famous old players including the 1957 Cup-winning heroes Johnny Dixon and Stan Lynn. Tickets for the game were purchased in advance and I was presented with a cheque by the then Villa chairman, Norman Smith.

A short while later I was in my bedroom, which was not unusual because after losing my sight I spent most of my time there listening to music. My collection of 600 or more pop records were a great source of encouragement, comfort and inspiration to me. Anyway, Mum came upstairs and knocked on my bedroom door – she didn't have to knock, of course, but people did that in those days out of respect and courtesy.

"John," Mum said, "you've got a visitor and you're never going to guess who it is".

"No, so who is it then?" I enquired inquisitively.

"It's Colin Withers and he's come straight from the Villa training ground, saying he read about you in the *Mail*."

Wow! I just shot downstairs as quickly as I could to meet one of my Aston Villa heroes. Colin Withers cut an imposing figure as befits a goalkeeper. He was a tall, muscular handsome guy, nicknamed 'Tiny' in keeping with typical football humour. He had signed for Aston Villa from our local rivals Birmingham City and ever since coming to the club he had been turning in impressive performances match after match and I was one of the many people who were chanting "Withers for England!" Now he had turned up at my house, but why?

Colin said he had been particularly touched by the newspaper article and could not begin to imagine what it must feel like to go blind, particularly for one so young and who loved playing and watching sport. We had a wonderful chat, drinking a few cups of Mum's incredible brew (tea for the uninitiated) and the time simply sped by. I learned that Colin was married and that he had two children. On leaving he said that he would call back the following week and we could go for a pub meal. Colin was true to his word and he arrived at my house with his wife Audrey and kids Mark and Sonia, who he said wanted to meet me. We all went for a meal at a pub called The Digby and it was great. There was such an ease of conversation though in the food stakes I chose something simple that would be easy to cut up and eat as that was still a big learning curve for me. Colin and I met on several occasions, but after he left Villa I am afraid I lost contact with him and would love to meet up again just to let him know what a great source of strength he was to me in those early days of disability.

A few weeks later I was to experience a strange twist of irony. I received a phone call from Ron Wylie, a former Aston Villa player now captain of Birmingham City. The irony was that Ron went to Birmingham in exchange for Colin Withers. Ron had been a big favourite at Villa Park since being signed by Eric Houghton from Notts County in 1958. Having played for Houghton as a youngster at Notts County, Ron had actually won the Midlands Player of the Year Award before moving on to Birmingham. I loved watching Ron play and a feature of his game was that he was able to create goal scoring opportunities for the likes of Gerry Hitchens, Peter McParland and Harry Burrows with his brilliant incisive passing. Later Ron was converted to be a wing half (midfielder in modern terms) where he was able to demonstrate his wonderful ability to tackle. Ron was not noted for being a prolific scorer, but he did occasionally chip in with some beauties.

Ron was phoning to ask if I would like to be his guest at the next Birmingham City home game, which I think was against Huddersfield Town. I gladly agreed, so Ron turned up at my parents' house a short while afterwards. Ron too had seen the same newspaper article that Colin Withers had seen and felt he wanted to do something to encourage me. We chatted non-stop in the car and when we arrived at St Andrews, Ron left me in the visitors' lounge and I was served a plate of sandwiches and the obligatory cup of tea. About half an hour later Ron re-emerged and took me down to the dressing room to meet his team-mates. Even though Birmingham was not my team, it was a real thrill to meet the likes of the talented centre forward Fred Pickering, Bert Murray and Barry Bridges who had signed from Chelsea, and the stylish Wales International Terry Hennessey. Ron then took me to the Press Box where I received a first-class commentary on the whole game, which for the record, Blues won 2-0.

After I had been to about three games Ron asked me how much I was enjoying the experience. I said it was great, but it would be even better if it was Villa! Ron expressed surprise that I was a Villa fan and, although I said that I mentioned it in the newspaper article, he said he could just not recall it. Ron apologised to me and half-jokingly said "I will never put you through this torture again!". Ron did, however, still have good connections at Villa Park and he arranged for me to be able to attend all Villa home games free and receive a commentary via the Birmingham Hospital Broadcasting Network (BHBN).

Once my first visit had been arranged, I turned up at about 2.15pm with my Dad, reporting to the Press Entrance. My Dad went off to take up his usual seat in the ground, while a man by the name of Reg Parton (who was a bit of a legend with the Press boys at Villa Park) looked after me. BHBN had a team of commentators who covered Birmingham City and Aston Villa games and I was introduced by Reg to the two people who would describe the game for me. Claire Newell and Geoff Pooke were on duty that day and they together with two other guys, Jack Hallam and David Wigley (later to work with BBC local radio) were to become good friends over the next few years.

Just before kick-off I was taken to my seat in the Press Box situated in the Trinity Road stand and I sat in the middle of three seats with a commentator either side. The person doing the commentary wore a set of headphones and so did I; it was all really exciting. During my years in the Press Box, I got to know one or two reporters including the well-known national writer Sam Leitch and my very favourite football writer Dennis Shaw. Dennis in fact once spotted me, white stick in hand, waiting for a bus in the Bromford Bridge area of Birmingham. He stopped, asked me where I was going and then gave me a lift in his car into the city centre.

They were indeed memorable days for me and I have Ron to thank for that. Ron is a really genuine man and we have remained good friends right through to the present time. Ron was once assistant to Gordon Milne at Coventry City. He was manager of West Bromwich Albion and at Aston Villa he was assistant to Vic Crowe and later became Community Relations Officer at the club. Ron, who has been happily married to Shirley for more years than we both care to remember, says that he really did not like management, but preferred working with players on a day to day basis in a coaching role.

Fancy that, though - two top players of their day reading a newspaper article and responding in such a kind and compassionate way. I would love to think the same kind of thing would happen today. Sportsmen and particularly footballers are so revered that they are in an incredibly privileged position to be able to help, encourage and inspire people.

Anyway, before I finish name dropping I have one more little surprise for you. While I had been away in Torquay on a rehabilitation course, learning to read Braille, to get around confidently using a white stick and to pick up basic typing skills, my family had been plotting a surprise for me. In the late 1960s, Aston Villa Football Club had undergone a revolution. They had almost gone out of business with massive debts, but the club had been saved by a takeover and a new shares issue. Doug Ellis took over as chairman from Norman Smith and the first thing he did was to appoint the high-profile and often controversial Tommy Docherty as our new manager. Incredibly our attendance figures soared from around 12,000 to over 40,000 overnight. A new broom had come in and swept everything clean and there was a new mood of optimism about the place. Tommy Docherty - or The Doc as he was popularly known - was a charismatic figure and the place was buzzing with anticipation. New signings Brian Tiler (tragically killed in a car accident a few years ago), Ian 'Chico' Hamilton, Pat McMahon and the Rioch brothers, Bruce and Neil came on board to hopefully herald a bright new dawn in the history of Aston Villa.

When I arrived home from Torquay I was greeted with my Dad's question, "You'll never guess who your Mother's been on the phone to". Tommy Docherty had responded to a request from my family and had rung up personally to invite me to the ground to meet him and his players. The date was arranged and I went along with my Dad. We sat in the manager's office for a short while with his secretary before Mr Docherty arrived. He shook our hands warmly and we chatted ninety to the dozen (where did that phrase come from?) while The Doc's secretary served up the coffee and biscuits. I specifically remember Tommy saying how amazed he had been by the crowds that were turning up and the wonderful welcome he had been given.

After a short time, he took us along to the dressing room, showed us how each player had his kit laid out and their special pegs for hanging clothes on. Soon the players started to arrive and my abiding memory is of chatting with our centre half at the time, John Sleeuwenhoek. John was the son of a Dutch paratrooper and in the local *Sports Argus* I remember seeing his photograph, accompanied by the words, "Say his name – slave en hook". John, also nicknamed 'Slogger', was tall, slim and blonde-haired. He was a quick and athletic centre half and one of the legendary Mercer Minors that I wrote about earlier. As other players began to arrive John would burst into song and the song that was on his lips, which I have to say he sang pretty well, but maybe not good enough for *Britain's Got Talent*, was Donovan's *Sunshine Superman*. Again, as with a number of these former players, John died tragically young, from a heart attack, at the age of 48.

As with Colin Withers and Ron Wylie before, it was a great thrill to meet some of my heroes and to have a little look at what goes on behind the scenes of a modern-day professional football club. A new era had begun, but it was not going to be all plain sailing, as Aston Villa were destined to nosedive into the depths of uncharted waters before they would eventually scale the heights once again. What an incredible rollercoaster ride we Villa supporters were going to embark upon during the next 15 years or so.

The euphoria which heralded Tommy Docherty's arrival was short-lived, as part way through his second season and with results disappointing, chairman Doug Ellis decided to pull the trigger and fire 'The Doc'. It was all so sad and I often wonder to this day whether the panic button was pushed too quickly. Tommy was great for the club; he created fresh excitement and also set up a youth policy which I believe we are seeing the benefits of to this day. However, Tommy was going to be replaced by the former Villa player and legend Vic Crowe. Vic could not keep us in Division Two, however, and we sank for the first time in our history to the old Division Three.

Relegation felt like the end of the world as a deep gloom fell over Aston Villa and its supporters. Just like many things in life, however, things did not turn out to be as bad as they felt at the time. Villa spent two years in the Third Division and eventful years they were, too. In the first season, we just missed out on promotion back to Division Two, but we did reach the League Cup Final, where we played the then all-conquering Tottenham Hotspur team at Wembley. I remember we got to the final by virtue of an exciting second leg 2-1 victory in the semi-final against Manchester United in front of a fanatical Villa Park crowd of just over 60,000. It was a floodlit game and I stood at the Holte End with my younger brother Paul, who was giving me a commentary, but who also was sadly to go blind a short while afterwards. The atmosphere was electric as we chanted "Villa-Villa-Villa" incessantly throughout the game. We roared the team on to a famous victory and I will never forget the wave of emotion when Pat McMahon's and Andy Lochhead's goals went in.

At the time of the final I had been blind for about four years and Paul and I travelled to Wembley on one of the supporters' coaches. We had a wonderful day in London and Villa played their full part in a terrific game. Although Spurs ran out 2-0 winners, courtesy of a brace from Martin Chivers, many of the neutrals felt that Villa had played well and were unlucky to lose. The likes of 'Chico' Hamilton, Bruce Rioch and skipper Brian Godfrey, driving us on from midfield, all had exceptional games.

The following season Villa stormed to the Third Division title with a record number of points and some great performances. I recall that we won 6-0 away to Oldham, for instance. The season was memorable for a number of reasons, not least because of our battle with Bournemouth at the top of the league. Bournemouth, then managed by the ex-West Ham United full back John Bond, were playing a brand of exciting attacking football that was way above their level. In Phil Boyer and Ted McDougall they had two strikers who were classy and the envy of many top sides in Division One. When Bournemouth came to Villa Park there was a crowd of nearly 50,000 plus the Match of the Day cameras to witness this top of the table battle in Division Three. On the day, Bournemouth were superb and no one present will ever forget the headed goal scored by Ted McDougall which ended in him gambolling into the net. The scene was shown on the opening credits of Match of the Day for a few years to come, because it was so spectacular.

I will always remember the amazing atmosphere at that match because, although Bournemouth led for much of the game, the Villa Park crowd roared so loud that they inspired their team to victory with two late goals from Andy Lochhead and Geoff Vowden. Villa goalkeeper at the time, Jimmy Cumbes, commented afterwards that he had never heard a noise like it, even at Old Trafford or Anfield. I just love games and atmospheres like that; they are all too rare nowadays I am afraid. At the end of an amazing season of high octane entertainment Bournemouth just missed out on promotion, finishing third in the table.

As I mentioned, Jimmy Cumbes was our goalkeeper in those days and he was a popular character for all kinds of reasons. Jim's engaging personality and happy-go-lucky approach to life gained him his own Sunday morning show on what was then BBC Radio Birmingham (now WM). Jim is also fondly remembered as being one of the last of the genuine all-round sportsmen who played professional football in the winter and cricket in the summer. As a right arm, fast medium bowler, he represented with distinction his home county of Lancashire (where he later went on to work as chief executive), Surrey, Worcestershire and Warwickshire. He also played football not just for Villa but also for Tranmere Rovers, West Bromwich Albion and Southport, as well as trying his hand in America by playing for Portland Timbers.

Although I am a Warwickshire cricket supporter, I have to say that our local rivals Worcestershire had quite a number of footballer/cricketers during that era. They included Ted Hemsley (Shrewsbury Town), Jim Standen (West Ham United and Luton Town), Phil Neal (Lincoln City) and later the great Sir Ian Botham. (Scunthorpe United)

Having achieved promotion from Division Three, the Aston Villa renaissance was well under way, but once we were back in Division Two, Vic Crowe's tenure as team manager was to be short-lived. Once again, we found ourselves struggling in the lower reaches of the league table. Surely Division Three could not be beckoning again? Well the Board of Directors must have feared so because less than 18 months after gaining promotion, the manager was sadly dismissed. Chairman, Doug Ellis, in his press conference to announce the decision said he did so with a heavy heart. Many of Doug's critics viewed that comment with a great deal of cynicism and it was around this time that journalists began to pick up on the expression 'Deadly Doug', a tag which, unfairly I think, stayed with Doug for the rest of his time at Villa Park. Curiously, as I understand, the term never did originally relate to a football matter. It was the legendary Jimmy Greaves, who nicknamed Doug 'deadly' after they had been salmon fishing together. Greaves picked up on this on one of his television appearances and Hey Presto! It stuck like glue to Mr Ellis from then on as far as the footballing fraternity were concerned.

In my dealings with Doug I have found him to be a very accommodating and highly personable bloke, always ready to help with a good cause or two and someone with a deeply held passion for Aston Villa Football Club. I loved the way he always called Aston Villa a family and as he once commented, "If I am such a tyrant to work for, why is it that so many of my staff have been with me for 20 years or more?" It's a good question and I have it on good authority from a number of ex-players that Doug often regarded them almost as sons and even after they had left the club he would still maintain a genuine interest in how they were doing. A number of the managers who were later 'sacked' (so called) by Doug still remain on good terms with him to this very day.

Many people believe the best thing Doug ever did was to sell the club to Randy Lerner and appoint Martin O'Neill as the manager. While I admit that both of those moves were excellent and in the best interests of the club, I think it's grossly unfair to treat the man who came in to rescue Aston Villa from oblivion in December 1968, with such disrespect.

Following the departure of Vic Crowe, the Board did pull a rabbit out of the hat for his replacement. Ron Saunders, the ex-Everton and Portsmouth centre forward, enjoyed success in taking Manchester City and Norwich City to successive League Cup Final victories at Wembley. No one could have envisaged what an inspired appointment this would turn out to be.

In his first season Ron Saunders took us to Wembley where we won the League Cup with a 1-0 win against his former club Norwich City, thanks to a late Ray Graydon goal. Former Villa goalkeeper Kevin Keelan brilliantly saved Graydon's penalty kick, but the winger was on hand to knock the rebound into the net. Ron Saunders had managed three different teams in consecutive seasons to the League Cup Final. Thankfully it was third time lucky with Villa, having lost in the two previous finals with Norwich City and Manchester City.

Saunders built another exciting Aston Villa side that would storm to the Division Two championship with some mesmerising attacking football. There were a number of outstanding players in that team and, while it is unfair on the others to mention one or two of them, I can't resist doing so. Right back John Gidman was one of the first overlapping full backs and his runs down the right wing were a joy to behold. John's pinpoint crosses were often met by the head of bustling centre forward Keith Leonard, a local lad who had been transformed by Ron from a run-of-the-mill reserve team player to someone who was feared by defenders throughout the country. Leonard's link-up play with the highly talented youngster Brian Little was to become legendary. Even though I never literally saw Brian Little with my own eyes, the anticipation that spread around the ground whenever he was on the ball was electrifying. Brian's mazy runs, dribbling ability and goal scoring exploits made him a firm favourite in the claret and blue shirt for years to come. Having secured top flight status after an absence of more than half a dozen years, Ron Saunders began to skilfully weld together a team that would in a few short years take Europe by storm.

Spearheaded by the mercurial talents of Brian Little (often compared in some ways to the genius of Trevor Francis, the emerging teenage sensation at Birmingham City), Villa powered their way to another League Cup triumph, this time against Everton. The game goes down in history because it is the only final (not sure if that's just in England or the entire world!) that took three matches to decide the outcome.

I went to Wembley again with my brother and two other friends for the first match, which resulted in a disappointing 0-0 stalemate. In fact, the match was so bad that ITV, who were scheduled to show highlights the following day, decided to drop the screening of it as there were no highlights. The replay was held at Hillsborough, home of Sheffield Wednesday and was only marginally better, finishing 1-1, with Bob Latchford equalising for Everton in the very last minute. As a result, a second replay was arranged and this took place at Old Trafford, home of Manchester United. Thankfully this was a much better and open game, with Villa winning 3-2. Chris Nicholl, Villa's commanding centre half, scored one of his very rare goals with a spectacular strike from 40 yards. The other two goals were scored, almost inevitably by Brian Little.

It was around this time Ron Saunders made two very significant signings for the Club. Two young Scotsmen arrived at Villa Park. Andy Gray was signed from Dundee United and Allan Evans came from Dunfermline Athletic. Both were centre forwards with reputations of being good headers of the football; it was thought that Evans would be the understudy to Gray, but it did not ultimately turn out that way. Ron Saunders masterfully transformed Evans into a centre half and he turned out to be one of the most effective defenders in the Club's long history, later forming a brilliant centre back partnership with yet another Scot, Ken McNaught.

It was at this time too that another young striker was coming through the junior ranks and I remember being at Villa Park to see him make his debut. John Deehan, formed a three-pronged strike force with Brian Little and Andy Gray, and for a season or two they struck fear into opposing defences, especially with the tricky Ray Graydon out on the right wing sending in immaculate crosses and chipping in with more than his fair share of goals. The game I referred to was against West Ham and was won 4-0 by Villa, with debutant Deehan scoring twice. That game paled into insignificance, however, when compared with a game I referred to in an earlier chapter.

Late in 1976 Liverpool came to Villa Park as reigning champions and conquering all before them in Europe. It was a Wednesday night and as always magic under the Aston Villa lights. In that first half, none of us present could actually believe what we were seeing. By half time with Villa playing some scintillating football we were 5-1 to the good with the goals being shared by the dynamic three up front, Gray, Little and Deehan. That turned out to be the end of the scoring, but no one present will ever forget that breath taking first-half performance, especially if they're Villa fans!

Chapter 6 - Heights of Glory

Ron Saunders was showing himself to be a wise master builder. He had put together a team which cruised out of the Second Division by playing the kind of exhilarating football that fills stadiums the world over. The mix of players was perfect with the flair players like John Gidman, Andy Gray, Brian Little and Alex Cropley being knit together alongside players with a strong work ethic epitomised by the non-stop running of Frank Carrodus.

Having achieved his goal of promotion, and given the time that group of players had had to bed into life at the higher level, Ron began the task of raising up a new team to make it assault on Division One and beyond. The signings of players like Dennis Mortimer (installed as captain), Des Bremner, Kenny Swain, Jimmy Rimmer and Tony Morley allied to the home-grown talent of Colin Gibson, Gary Williams, Gordon Cowans and Gary Shaw ensured that Villa, for the time being at least, would not be battling to stave off yet another relegation. In fact, Villa's stock began to rise and their attractive football caused pundits from around the country to sit up and take notice.

Ron Saunders would perform one more master-stroke before his latest team creation was complete. He dipped into the transfer market and signed the much-travelled Peter Withe to form a new striking partnership with the new young scoring sensation Gary Shaw. It has been said this was a marriage made in heaven because Withe and Shaw hit it off right from the start and each one benefitted the other's game. Peter Withe had been a journeyman footballer with many clubs, but had really blossomed at Nottingham Forest under the astute guidance of Brian Clough and Peter Taylor. He had then moved on to Newcastle United, where it was assumed he would see out his career – until the Ron Saunders stroke of genius that is!

The rest is history. In the 1980/81 campaign Villa, using only 14 players for the entire season, were consistency itself and ran out League Division One Champions, just pipping Bobby Robson's highly talented Ipswich Town side to the title. Many do not feel Villa received the credit they deserved that season for winning the Championship as the majority of neutrals favoured Ipswich and, fair play to them, they did play a very attractive style of football. During the course of the season Villa did lose twice to Ipswich, once under the Villa Park lights in a pulsating game that briefly took Ipswich back to the top of the table with only a few games remaining. Villa, however, pushed on from there and eventually won the day to achieve their first championship in more than 70 years.

This fantastic achievement meant that Villa qualified to represent England in the European Cup, a competition which had been dominated by English clubs for the previous five years or so, with Liverpool and Nottingham Forest winning the coveted trophy year in year out. The Villa team struggled in the league the following season finding it hard to recapture the consistency of their title-winning campaign. Europe was a different matter though and they progressed through the early rounds to get to the quarter-finals without too much difficulty. Nothing, however, could prepare the players or the fans for the hammer blow that was about to strike. Ron Saunders resigned and walked out of the club after a disagreement of some description with the Board. Doug Ellis was not chairman at this time as he had been ousted from the Board, and it is a source of great regret to Doug that he was not in charge during Villa's glory days of the early 1980s.

Assistant Manager Tony Barton was thrust into the limelight and took charge of Villa's league and European campaigns. The league position stabilised somewhat, but the European adventure went from strength to strength, until unbelievably Villa were into the final where they would meet German giants, Bayern Munich.

On that balmy May evening in Rotterdam in 1982 thousands of Villa fans arrived hoping and praying for a miracle. Well, as you well know, the miracle actually happened. Although being outplayed territorially for most of the game, Villa won courtesy of that Peter Withe goal in the second half when a cross from Tony Morley went into the Bayern net off his shin.

The Villa men battled and defended stoutly throughout and of course the match was an amazing triumph for young goalkeeper Nigel Spink, who had previously only played one first team game. He was brought on to the field after less than 10 minutes after a neck injury sustained by the regular keeper Jimmy Rimmer. Spink turned in the performance of his life to keep a clean sheet; no mean feat against the German hotshots. I sat at home and took in the whole experience with the television on, the video recorder going and with at least two radios on, taping the commentary from different radio channels. *Oh, what a night* someone once put into a song, but that incredible night in 1982 is one which I and thousands of other Aston Villa supporters will never forget as long as we live.

I mentioned that Ron Saunders was, in management terms, a wise master builder and the reason why at this point I was not attending Aston Villa games was because I had met someone else who was described as a wise master builder. This man's name is Jesus Christ and I had become a committed Christian. By that I simply mean that I was in it for real. It was not an add-on to my life, but when I gave my life to Jesus Christ I came to the point of believing that He had died for me upon the Cross all those years ago, and had been raised from the dead. Having given Him my life and asked Him to forgive my sins, as a wise master builder, He was now reconstructing my life in such a way as to bring glory to Him. I was now living my life to do His will, and after all these years my faith and passion for Jesus has never diminished but in fact grown stronger as I learned to rely upon Him for everything, literally. My spiritual journey is documented in great detail in my book *Fear, Fun and Faith'*.

For a while, I thought that giving all of me – my life, my heart and my soul – to Jesus meant that I would not be going to see Villa again, but in essence what it meant was that Aston Villa would no longer be the God of my life. Aston Villa would fall in line behind Jesus and my family. As a result, and, over a period of time, I began to serve God by being active in my local church and also in going to meetings to tell the story of how I came to faith.

There was one incredible afternoon when, for me, faith and football came together in one. My wife Sylvia had driven me to Maney Hill School in Sutton Coldfield where I was to speak at an after-school bible class. As we drove into the car park Sylvia could see into the school hall and she said there was a man showing a trophy to the school kids. We got out of the car and walked closer and Sylvia said, "You are never going to believe this, but that's Tony Barton, the Villa manager".

Sylvia was right, I did not believe it, but having spoken to Mrs Waller, the teacher who ran the bible class, she confirmed that this was actually the Villa manager and he had brought the European Cup to show the children. My eyes opened wide with excited anticipation and the teacher asked if I would like to meet Tony Barton. It was, of course, a silly question and it was only a few minutes before I was talking with Tony and actually holding the European Cup. I was shocked how heavy it was and asked how players could have the energy, after 90 minutes of hard graft, to run around the pitch carrying it. Tony said that when you have just won the European Cup you could climb Everest and I got the point. What a thrill though to get my hands on that prestigious piece of silverware!

Chapter 7 - The Only Way is Down!

Having climbed the summit, there is only one way to go from there and that is down, but no one could have predicted that Villa's fall from grace would be as dramatic as its rise had been.

Within a year or so of winning the European Cup, Tony Barton, a genial gentleman, if ever there was one, was fired due to indifferent results. By now Doug Ellis who had been steadily buying up shares in the club, had regained his role as chairman and the Board appointed Graham Turner as Tony Barton's successor. It transpired that Tony Barton died suddenly from a heart attack not too long afterwards.

This was a source of great sadness to Tony's family and many friends inside the game. I had the privilege of attending Tony's funeral service at Aston Parish Church, which clearly demonstrated the high regard in which he was held. After the service, I enjoyed some light refreshments in the company of two Villa League and European Cup-winning legends in Colin Gibson and Des Bremner. They were accompanied by Reverend David Carr, then working for the Professional Footballers' Association on player pensions. Many years later, my wife and I began attending Renewal Christian Centre in Solihull, which is the church David Carr and his wife Molly pioneered over 40 years ago. They now have a congregation of over 1,500 people and include in their number quite a few former and current professional footballers. These include the likes of Cyrille Regis, Andy Sinton, Darren Moore, Derek Jefferson, Denis Bailey and James Chambers.

Graham Turner had gained a reputation as a bright young coach with Shrewsbury Town, where he had also been a player of great distinction for many years. Graham was only at the Villa for a couple of years or so, but in that time, I got to know him quite well. It was during his time at the helm that the Heysel Stadium disaster took place and I remember all too clearly hearing the BBC Radio commentary as the story was unfolding. Peter Jones (one of my all-time favourite football commentators) was describing the awful scenes before him with Emlyn Hughes providing the summaries.

What they described was so graphic and appalling that it was as though a deep knot was forming in my stomach. I struggled for a while to hold back the tears as the scene of death and destruction began to emerge. I began to feel a sense of shame and disgust at even being English and to be associated with what were wrongly being labelled as 'football hooligans'. They were in fact hooligans who just happened to attach themselves to our beautiful game and they were ugly symptoms of the sick society we were creating.

In the grief that I was feeling I resolved never to go to another professional football game. I just did not want to be associated with this kind of thuggery. It was all getting worse and horribly out of hand. Of course, in the days that followed there were all kinds of voices being heard, many of them totally outrageous in their views, ranging from bringing back corporal punishment to capital punishment and everything in between. I am not totally opposed to capital punishment, but we can argue that one at another time and in another place.

Anyway, I was in church just a few days later and as we were singing a song of praise to God it was as though I heard a voice within me and it said, "Let your voice be heard above that of the heathen".

Quite a strange phrase, I think you'll agree. Well I was convinced that this was God speaking to me and as I mulled the phrase over in the next day or two and spoke with people whose opinions I valued, it became clear that God did not want me to stop going to football, but he wanted me to play a role, however small, in trying to clean it up.

Some years earlier I had undertaken a research project and through it I had discovered that a healthy percentage of our professional football clubs had started off life in the Christian Church, often as men's bible classes back in the 19th century. That was certainly the case with Aston Villa who were originally Aston Villa Wesleyan Chapel. I am really proud of the Christian roots of Aston Villa Football Club and of its reputation as being family-friendly. Just as an aside, tradition says that the men who formed Aston Villa Football Club did so under a lamp post in Heathfield Road, Handsworth. Just so happens I was born at the maternity hospital in that very same road; a few years later though you understand!

Now I was feeling that God wanted me to take the club back to its roots and form a Christian Supporters Association. I wrote to the Club's Commercial Manager, Tony Stephens, and asked if I could meet for a chat. Tony readily agreed and I joined him one morning in his office. I related my idea to Tony and he called the chairman, Doug Ellis, in to hear what I had to say and both were quite sympathetic to my ideas.

The plan was to gather together as many Aston Villa supporters who were happy to call themselves Christians as possible and to meet for one hour before every home match to pray. We would pray for a good and positive atmosphere in the ground, for a sporting game of football and that the fans would appreciate skill on the field, whichever side it came from. We also prayed for players that their behaviour would be exemplary, for any who were injured (short or long term) and for their families. In addition, we wanted to gather as many as possible who had this positive outlook, to stand together at the famous Holte End of the ground so we could create a positive atmosphere where we were and then pray that that would spread. We would refrain from booing, personally slagging off players or singing obscene songs. It was on this basis, therefore, that the Aston Villa Christian Supporters Association was born. We received brilliant support from the club, not least of all from manager Graham Turner, whose wife Anne and two sons also attended some of our prayer meetings.

Following the tragedy at the Heysel Stadium, a band of about 15 Christians from a variety of church backgrounds, met together at a small Anglican Church in Bevington Road, Aston to pray. It was during one of those prayer meetings that an idea was born which we needed to put before the Aston Villa hierarchy.

I duly arranged to have lunch with Graham Turner along with one of his assistants, Malcolm Beard, and put the idea to them. The thought was that instead of the two teams coming on to the field separately to a mixed sound of cheers and boos, it would be better if the teams came out of the dressing rooms and on to the field side by side. In that way, the overall sound would be a positive one with both sets of fans cheering their heroes on to the pitch. This kind of entrance had happened for years with FA Cup Finals and international matches, so why not in domestic league games?

Both Graham and Malcolm liked the idea and said they would put it to the chairman and opposing team's officials once the new fixtures were out. Well, would you believe it? When those fixtures were released a few days later, Villa's first home game would be against none other than Liverpool. The end result was that on that memorable August evening Aston Villa and Liverpool players came out side by side to a rapturous reception from a nearly full house. As those of us from the prayer group stood at the Holte End we felt really proud at the positive atmosphere which was created. Slowly but surely, this practice began to spread around the country so that now it is commonplace for teams to come out side by side, maybe the world over. It is so nice to know we achieved something that is of value in the modern game. At the end of that season Aston Villa supporters won the Bertie Bassett award for having the most sporting fans. I think we and the Almighty took just a little credit for that!

For the record, that game against Liverpool finished 2-2 with Ian Rush for Liverpool and Mark Walters for Aston Villa, scoring two goals apiece. This was also the game where I took my then seven-year-old son Ian along for the first time thus carrying on the family tradition. Thankfully Ian has gone on to become as big an Aston Villa supporter as me, some 30 years later. Just shows, it's Villa in the blood!

Following the publicity we received in the press and on local radio, a number of other Christian supporters around the country got in touch to enquire how they could go about starting similar groups for their clubs. I remember having chats with supporters who called me from Charlton Athletic and Portsmouth for instance, but I do not know what came of their interest. I do know that a prayer group formed at Birmingham City, however, under the leadership of a local Christian musician, Roger Jones, who happened to be a keen Birmingham City fan and just as concerned about the negative image surrounding professional football as I had been.

My wife and I did experience one very unsavoury incident around this time. I had been out at a church meeting, but on my return Sylvia was clearly distressed. She had received a phone call from someone asking for me. He was very well spoken and said he was from the 'Zulu warriors', which are part of the hooligan element which attaches itself to Birmingham City. When Sylvia told him I was out, he said to tell me that if I ever set foot anywhere near the St Andrews ground again they would kill me. We notified the police and that is the last we have heard of it, but it does give you some idea of what we are dealing with out there, doesn't it?

After about three years, with my move to Cornwall and the sudden premature death of my successor, John Gosnall, the Aston Villa prayer group ceased to exist. In 2015, however, I felt stirred to launch a new prayer group with friends and fellow football supporters Mark Leonard and Geoff Kyte linked to my local church. Currently there is a small group of us meeting up for an hour on the first Saturday of every month to pray for all aspects of Aston Villa Football Club and its employees. Even though things appear to have deteriorated since we began praying, thus opening ourselves up to much ridicule, nevertheless we feel confident that our prayers are being heard and that we, as a Club, will again scale the heights and become a real force for good in the worldwide football family. As I said previously, Aston Villa began life as part of the Wesleyan Chapel and so it feels entirely appropriate that we should now be praying from a church base that has the legendary John and Charles Wesley at its very foundation. We are very happy to welcome other Aston Villa supporters to be part of our prayer group. Likewise, it would be great to hear of supporters of other clubs in the UK or around the world who are meeting together to pray.

While the Graham Turner era saw the removal of many of the League Championship and European Cup winning heroes we did see the emergence of a few other stars. England international Steve Hodge signed from Nottingham Forest, Paul Rideout, a young striker came with a big reputation, French international left winger Didier Six arrived at the club and straight from our youth set up emerged local talent Mark Walters; the best since Brian Little, many people

View of Villa Park approaching from Aston Park (pre 1958)

View from the Witton End during a match at Villa Park (pre 1958). To me the atmosphere was just electric!

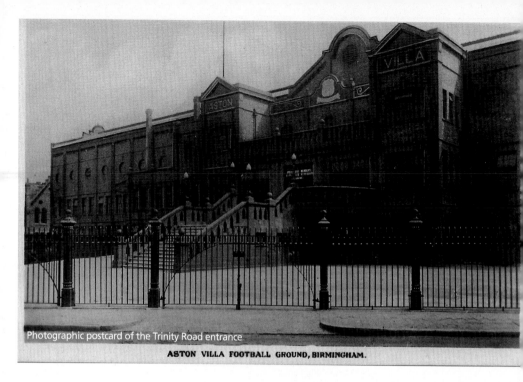

Photographic postcard of the Trinity Road entrance

ASTON VILLA FOOTBALL GROUND, BIRMINGHAM.

The Trinity Road entrance steps (Aug 1985)

ASTON VILLA.F.C. — F.A.CUP WINNERS 1956-7

Mr.F.J.Archer Mr.F.B.Normansell Mr.W.E.Houghton S.Lynn N.Sims Mr.N.L.Smith S.Crowther W.Moore
Secretary Director Team-Manager Director Trainer
Mr.J.Broughton J.Sewell W.Myerscough Mr.C.S.Buckley J.Dixon P.Aldis Mr.W.E.Lovesey
Vice-Chairman Chairman Captain Director
L.Smith J.Dugdale F.A. CUP P.Saward P.McParland

ASTON VILLA FOOTBALL CLUB 1959-60

P.Aldis S.Lynn J.Dugdale W.Beaton N.Sims T.Birch P.McParland G.Hitchens

R.Shaw P.Saward R.Thomson V.Crowe J.Dixon L.Smith Mr.J.Mercer
Trainer Manager
J.Adam J.Sewell J.MacEwan R.Wylie J.Neale

ASTON VILLA FOOTBALL CLUB 1960-61
FIRST WINNERS OF THE FOOTBALL LEAGUE CUP

A.O'Neill H.Burrows J.McEwan G.Sidebottom A.Deakin J.Neal R.Brown

J.Mercer R.Shaw R.Wylie S.Lynn N.Sims G.Lee J.Dugdale R.Thomson F.J.Archer
Manager Trainer Secretary
Mr.J.Heath Mr.N.Smith V.Crowe Mr.C.S.Buckley P.McParland Mr.F.B.Normansell Mr.W.E.Lovesey
Director Director Captain Chairman Vice-Captain Director Director
THE FOOTBALL LEAGUE CUP

Top:
A jubilant Aston Villa team in their dressing room after defeating Manchester United 2-1 to win the FA Cup in May 1957

Above:
Bringing home the FA Cup! I will never forget the atmosphere surrounding Villa Park when the team took to the streets on their victory parade

Left:
Johnny Dixon and Peter McParland show the FA Cup to the Mayor during formal celebrations (May 1957)

A rare colour photograph of the 1957 FA Cup winning line-up

Stan Lynn scores a penalty as part of a hat trick. Aston Villa 5 - Sunderland 2 (11 January 1958)

Wally Hazelden beats his man - Aston Villa 3 - Burnley 0 (8 March 1958)

Villa Park with open terraces, prior to the Holte End development and roof in 1962

Peter McParland, aged 22, Aston Villa professional as well as Irish International (c1956)

George Lunn - Aston Villa
He played once for Aston Villa in a friendly during World War 2. He was my coach in Sunday League football

Charlie Aitken of Aston Villa (Aug 1959 - May 1976

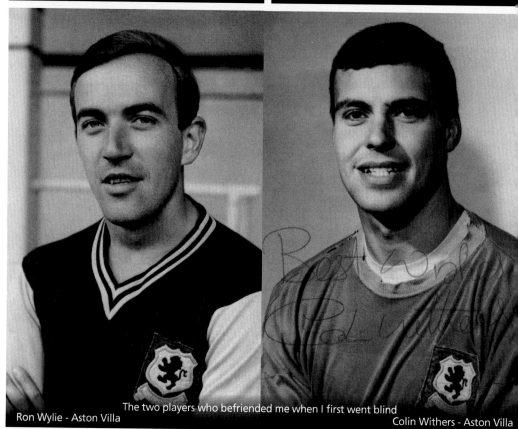

The two players who befriended me when I first went blind

Ron Wylie - Aston Villa

Colin Withers - Aston Villa

Arthur Sabin - Aston Villa

Charlie Aitken - Aston Villa

Brian Little - Aston Villa

Andy Gray - Aston Villa

Dean Saunders - Aston Villa

Dwight Yorke - Aston Villa

Dion Dublin - Aston Villa

Olof Mellberg - Aston Villa

John Carew - Aston Villa

Danny Blanchflower of Tottenham
Hotspur and Northern Ireland

Ronnie Allen of West Bromwich
Albion and England

Bobby Robson of West Bromwich
Albion and England

Some of the many players I admired from other teams

Gil Merrick -
Birmingham City

Adam Blacklaw -
Burnley

Nat Lofthouse -
Bolton Wanderers

Peter Broadbent -
Wolves & Aston Villa

Alex Elder -
Burnley

Bryan Douglas -
Blackburn Rovers

Bobby Moore -
West Ham and England

Ian St. John -
Liverpool and Scotland

Y FOUR BIG MACS of Aston Villa - Top left: Peter McParland (1952-1962), Top right: Pat McMahon (1969–1976)
Bottom left: Alan McInally (1987–1989), Bottom right: Paul McGrath (1989–1996)

European Cup Winners in Rotterdam on 26 May 1982, Dennis Mortimer and Peter Withe exit the plane holding the cu
Sometime later, I was to find out how heavy it was when I got to lift it too!

Christian Benteke - Aston Villa

60 years on...
Peter McParland with the
iconic FA Cup-Winner's shirt
of 1957

Inset bottom left:
...and me, re-living that
glorious victory!

Peter McParland's 1957 FA Cup winners medal.

Peter's display of FA Cup original
photographs from 1957

A day I will never forget! The FA Cup Final 2015 at Wembley Stadium, when I finally got to meet my life-long hero, Peter McParland

With Peter McParland before the match at Wembley Stadium 30 May 2015. A new friendship began

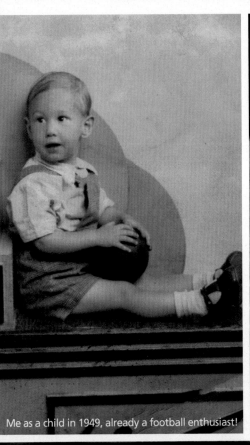

Me as a child in 1949, already a football enthusiast!

At our family home in Erdington, aged 11.
My passion for 'The beautiful game' had clearly begun

All kitted out, with my son Ian, for the Aston Villa v Chelsea FA Cup Final in 2000

John pitch-side at Villa Park in May 2015

What an honour to be invited to my beloved Villa Park for a personal tour by CEO Tom Fox, May 2015

Ian and I relax before the 2015 FA Cup Final at Wembley

As one of Villa's most loyal supporters, I was interviewed by Ben Chapman for ITV National News, prior to the 2015 FA Cup Final

said. None of these players, however, could work the oracle and turn Aston Villa into a major force again and with us languishing just below mid-table the chop fell on Graham Turner just as it had on some of his illustrious predecessors.

Graham left on good terms and the general feeling was that this was a job that came too soon for someone so inexperienced at the highest level. Graham Turner later joined Wolverhampton Wanderers as their manager and went on to be one of their most successful managers of all time; not least of all because he signed the now legendary Steve Bull from their Black Country rivals West Bromwich Albion along with Andy Thompson, who also turned out to be a fan favourite at Molineux. Turner also snapped up Andy Mutch who went on to form a formidable and subsequently legendary striking partnership with Steve Bull for years to come.

Who would be next in line for the hot seat at Villa Park? Well, it was the former Celtic and Scotland centre half and captain Billy McNeill. This appeared to be a universally popular appointment with supporters and the media alike. Billy's track record as a player and a manager were second to none and this time the much-maligned Villa Board had gone for the big name that fans had been clamouring for. Regrettably, however, it all went disastrously wrong.

Villa were relegated back to Division Two at the end of that season and McNeill left the club by mutual consent. For whatever reasons, the move had simply not worked out and just five years after winning Europe's biggest prize Villa were now dumped back into the second tier of English football. The critics were out in force now and many shareholders and local radio sports presenters, as well as the everyday supporters, were holding Doug Ellis personally responsible for this rapid fall down the football ladder.

At this point, enter Graham Taylor. Under the chairmanship of rock star and lifelong fan Elton John, Watford Football Club had come from near obscurity to gain successive promotions to Division One. Under the wise management of Graham Taylor, Watford had turned in some memorable performances, especially in the cup competitions and they had spawned some bright new stars in the process. Most notable of these was John Barnes who went on to achieve outstanding success with Liverpool and England with his wizardry out on the left wing. The Hornets had a lethal striking partnership too with Ross Jenkins and Luther Blissett being on hand to capitalise on the superb service they receive from Barnes on the left and Nigel Callaghan on the right. Welsh International Kenny Jackett was another of the many hard-working players who epitomised the Watford team of those days.

It must have been a hard decision to leave Watford at the height of their success, but Mr Taylor came to Villa amid a blaze of publicity. It wasn't, I have to say, a universally popular choice, because some people (ignorantly in my view) labelled Taylor's style of football as being 'long ball' and not attractive enough. But Graham made an immediate impact on the club and with a host of new players took us to promotion back to the top flight of English football. After a tough first season back in the old First Division, we scaled the heights the following campaign and rose to the dizzy heights of runners up. History reveals that during his time at the club, Graham Taylor signed players who would later be described as legends of Aston Villa. Just take a look at this for an impressive list of signings:

• David Platt was bought from Crewe Alexandra for £200,000. He went on to play many games for Villa, gained England caps and then was sold to Italian club Bari for £5.5m, a record at the time for an outgoing Villa player.

• Dwight Yorke was spotted as a young boy in Trinidad by Graham Taylor and Doug Ellis when Villa were on a pre-season tour. Dwight was invited over to England for a trial and I guess you know the rest. Dwight, who cost the princely sum of £10,000 went on to have a memorable career before moving on to Manchester United for a nice fat fee of £12.6m to boost the Villa Park coffers. At Old Trafford he performed with great distinction, forming a lethal goal-scoring partnership with Andy Cole.

• Alan McInally was signed from Celtic for a fee of £225,000. 'Rambo' as he was nicknamed by the Villa fans for his rampaging no-nonsense approach, soon became a crowd favourite as he scored some spectacular goals. After just two seasons at the club, during which time he achieved cult status, Alan moved on to Bayern Munich for a £1.1m fee.

• Paul McGrath was surely the greatest (certainly from the fans perspective) of all of Graham Taylor's signings. Despite his much-publicised knee problems and his regular binge drinking sessions (talked about in his own autobiography), Paul did not miss many matches for Villa. His positional sense, classic reading of the game, class and elegance were a joy to behold, or at least so I am told. When 'God' (as he has been dangerously dubbed) was on the ball, I often heard the collective intake of breath at the sheer genius of this man.

Thank you, Graham, for giving us these legends to remember and talk about for the rest of our lives. I have to say though, it was not just this famous and fabulous quartet that mark Graham Taylor out as one of the finest managers in the transfer market I have ever come across.

There were many other players he signed during his first tenure at the club who gave great value for money, contributing fully to the team work ethic and became big fan favourites. How many of you for instance remember the contributions of Kevin Gage (bought from Wimbledon and what a shot he had on him), Stuart Gray (who became captain and was a true gentleman) Derek Mountfield (an ever-reliable centre half signed from Everton and with a real eye for goal), Kent Nielsen (the towering Danish defender) and Ian Ormondroyd (a most unlikely looking footballer, tall in the extreme and nicknamed 'Sticks' by the fans). These players together with the ever-reliable Nigel Spink, still going strong in goal, and other home grown players such as the classy Gordon Cowans, the silky skills of Mark Walters, the lightning quick Tony Daley and the often-underrated Ian Olney.

Less impressive was one of Graham's other signings. He went back to Watford to secure the services of Nigel Callaghan, which at the time seemed like a good move all around. Unfortunately, however Nigel incurred the wrath of the Villa supporters by first of all turning in some tepid performances, which led to him being (I think unfairly) booed and then in one particular match it was perceived by many that he pulled out of a 50-50 tackle. This was deemed to be unforgiveable by passionate fans and really after that his days at Villa were numbered and he left the club without ever making the mark I feel he should have done.

In that incredible title-challenging season David Platt was sensational in his attacking midfield role and this led to not only an England call up, but also to him being transferred to Italian Club Bari the following year. In addition, England were on the lookout for a new manager and the Football Association came knocking at our door to speak to Graham Taylor about the vacancy. The Board made the only decision that was open to them really and after brief talks,

Graham Taylor, our most successful manager by far since Ron Saunders, was on his way to manage the national side. Yet again Aston Villa were without a manager so where would the Board look this time? No one could have guessed the surprise that was in store and as the Press Conference came around Doug Ellis pulled another of his proverbial rabbits out of the hat!

Chapter 8 - Onwards and Upwards

The decade of the 1990s was destined to be a pretty good one for the Villans and to say it started off interestingly is an understatement. Following the departure of Graham Taylor to manage England, the Board moved swiftly to appoint his successor, but no one could have predicted who that man would be. Of course, today foreign managers and coaches are commonplace, especially in the Premier League, but in those days, it was almost totally unheard of. Doug Ellis, however, proudly announced to the shocked media that our next manager would be the Czech born, Dr Jo Venglos, who came to the Club with the best of credentials as a top coach, respected across the football world. The story was told that the much-respected Bobby Robson recommended Dr Jo to the Villa Board.

Dr Jo (or Dr No, as the Press dubbed him) was a gentle and quietly spoken man who was apparently an astute tactician. In hindsight, I think the gamble was a good one. It could so easily have come off, but it didn't and after one season he was dismissed. The team struggled throughout their league campaign and, while not in any immediate danger of relegation, Villa did not achieve the high level of performance that the Board and the fans desired. We did have a decent run in the UEFA cup, however, and there was a memorable game at Villa Park against Inter Milan, which resulted in a 2-0 victory for Villa with superb goals from Kent Nielsen and David Platt.

Throughout the 92 Football League clubs it struck me that the average shelf life of a manager was around two to three years. After all, there are only so many team talks you can give and I suppose players just get weary and cease responding to the same old expletives day after day delivered from the same voice. The words, I guess, just lose their power. It must take a really great manager with some superb motivational skills to get the same group of players at it season after season. That is why Sir Alex Ferguson, love him or loathe him, must be the greatest football manager of all time. To have done what he did for well over 20 years with Manchester United is nothing short of amazing.

In my years of following Aston Villa, we have certainly followed the trend of chopping and changing managers and Dr Jo was followed by the flamboyant Ron Atkinson. You may recall from my earlier recollections that I had seen Ron as a young man playing in the Villa reserves before he moved on to do sterling service with Oxford United. As a manager, Ron had developed a reputation for producing teams that played expansive, attractive football and he had managed with some success at West Bromwich Albion and Manchester United. At the Albion in particular, he had a team full of panache with plenty of goals in it. They entertained wherever they played and of course that side contained what became known as 'The Three Degrees'. Brendon Batson, Laurie Cunningham and Cyrille Regis, were named after the black girl singing group of the same name.

I actually wrote to Brendon Batson on a particular occasion after he had sustained a career-threatening injury. I was really impressed by his attitude in adversity so I wrote to say so and also said I would be praying for him. I said how important prayer was to me and especially at that time as one of my young daughters, Allison, had been seriously injured in a car accident. Just a few days later Allison received a beautiful card from Brendon, signed by all of the West Bromwich Albion players. I will never forget that act of kindness, which I believe is so typical of the man. More about my letter writing activities later.

Laurie Cunningham, a magnificently exciting right winger of the old school was tragically killed in a car accident in Spain a few years later and this had a profound effect on his close friend Cyrille Regis. The heart searching that Cyrille did following the premature death of his pal, led eventually to him becoming a Christian; what the media often now describe as 'born again'. Cyrille, who is now a football agent, has grown in his faith and is a very able communicator, regularly being invited to speak at Church-based or Christians in Sport events.

Meanwhile at Villa Park, Ron Atkinson was getting his feet under the table and even though his time in the hot seat was not to be much longer than any of his predecessors, the time he was there was tremendously exciting. I, along with many other Aston Villa fans, regard those days under 'Big Ron' as some of the most thrilling days we have witnessed as Villa supporters.

When Ron Atkinson went looking for new players to bring in, it was reported by a journalist that he went shopping in Harrods rather than Aldi. For instance, he went to Liverpool and bought the likes of established International players such as Steve Staunton, Ray Houghton and Dean Saunders. He bought another experienced international player from Chelsea in Andy Townsend and went to Spain to pick up the former Everton and Arsenal player Kevin Richardson, who was then appointed by Ron as captain of the team.

Ron also purchased a new centre forward in Dalian Atkinson. Dalian was somewhat of an enigma to say the least. Brilliant on his day and able to terrorise defences with his great pace, power and shooting ability. Unfortunately, there was something in Dalian's temperament that prevented him going on to fulfil his undoubted potential. Full back Earl Barrett was also brought in as was a surprise signing. Cyrille Regis, then approaching the veteran stage, came in from Coventry City on a free transfer and gave a couple of years' excellent service to the club. Goalkeeper Mark Bosnich and the rapidly improving Dwight Yorke also stepped up from the reserve team to take their place in a very exciting football team.

With the players at his disposal Ron Atkinson was able to get us to second place in the inaugural season of the newly formed Premier League. He also took us to our first League Cup triumph in 15 years. Aston Villa defeated one of Big Ron's former clubs, Manchester United at Wembley by 3-1 with two goals from Dean Saunders and one from Dalian Atkinson. It was a superb performance by the Villa boys and I was thrilled to be there at Wembley with my son Ian.

The day itself was remarkable for Ron's shock team selection. Ray Houghton was surprisingly left out of the starting line up in favour of young Graham Fenton, who had only played a handful of first team games at the time. The selection was hailed as a tactical masterclass by Big Ron as Villa's five-man midfield (including Fenton) stifled United's flair players.

The Ron Atkinson days were memorable ones indeed and it came as a surprise and a disappointment to many supporters when he was sacked following a defeat at Wimbledon. The reason given by Doug Ellis for this unpopular dismissal was that a run of something like six or seven wins out of more than forty in the previous 12 months was unacceptable. I think most of us were surprised by those statistics as by and large we were enjoying the football and the quality of the players on view. So it was that Ron departed, amid some bitter words, which hopefully with the passage of time have healed somewhat.

I have already written about the exploits of Brian Little as a player – a true and much loved Aston Villa legend. Now, however, it was his turn to try and bring long lasting success to the football club in a managerial role. Brian arrived from Leicester City with his assistant Allan Evans (from the great team of the late seventies and early eighties) and first team coach John Gregory (another ex- player from the Ron Saunders days). Unfortunately, this move was filled with acrimony because Leicester did not want to lose their management team. Brian Little, however, resigned saying that Aston Villa had a special place in his heart, having been there since he was a boy.

Again, as with Ron beforehand, Brian Little's time in management at Villa Park was relatively successful. With the side playing some attractive football we climbed to fourth and fifth place in the Premier League and two years after 'Big Ron's' Wembley success, Brian Little took us back there where Villa defeated Leeds United 3-0 in another superb display. Goals from Dwight Yorke, Savo Milosevic and Ian Taylor, ensure that the claret and blue army went back to Birmingham deliriously happy.

Two of Brian Little's signings stood out and epitomised his team. Gareth Southgate came in from Crystal Palace as a midfield player, but he was soon converted to a very effective and classy centre back, where he performed with distinction for Villa and subsequently England. Alongside Ugo Ehiogu and the young Gareth Barry, Southgate formed one of the best defensive partnerships in the Premier League. Ian Taylor, who was to become one of Villa's most popular players, was brought in from Sheffield Wednesday in exchange for striker Guy Whittingham. Brian brought in three players, at no little expense, who though very talented in their own right, were to create problems for him in one way or another. Serbia International Savo Milosevic (who formed a more than useful strike force with Dwight Yorke), Sasa Curcic and Stan Collymore all made valuable contributions to the team at different points, but at the same time posed a series of disciplinary headaches for the manager, which ultimately took their toll and Brian Little dramatically resigned after three years in charge, saying that he needed a break as he was mentally shattered. It was a disappointing end to what had been a pretty successful few seasons following in the footsteps of the flamboyant Ron Atkinson.

The managerial merry-go-round was in full swing now at Villa Park, as with other clubs in fairness, and the next appointment was to meet with almost universal disapproval and criticism by fans and media alike. John Gregory, who by then had left the club to become manager of Wycombe Wanderers was given the job of helping Villa to continue as a top Premier League team. By and large, apart from the occasional season, the 1990s had seen Villa hovering around the top six fairly consistently. Now John Gregory had been given the task of pushing us on to achieve even more. The nub of the criticism being levelled at Doug Ellis and the rest of the Board was that they were lacking in ambition and by appointing the inexperienced John Gregory they were going for the cheapest option.

Once again, however, we continued to do reasonably well. As with Ron Atkinson and Brian Little's teams before him John Gregory's players turned in some entertaining displays and overall the fans were happy with what they were seeing and the results being achieved. Some of John Gregory's better signings were Mark Delaney (a young right back from Cardiff City), Olof Mellberg (a Sweden international centre back), Dion Dublin (from Coventry City) and Paul Merson (who arrived from Middlesbrough for £6.75m).

One of John Gregory's most remembered feats was that he managed to get Aston Villa into the FA Cup Final for the first time in 43 years. We played in the last FA Cup Final at the old Wembley Stadium.

The match was an instantly forgettable drab game which Villa lost 1-0 to Chelsea, but it was a very emotional day for me because I was there once again with my son Ian. That in itself may not sound so remarkable, but only a couple of years beforehand we had almost lost Ian. He had been taken suddenly ill with a brain virus called Encephalitis, and Ian's life hung in the balance for two or three days, but when he did turn the corner, the surgeon said that he had made a spectacular recovery. Hundreds of people around the country had been praying for Ian's wellbeing and so not for the first time we felt indebted to our many friends and full of thankfulness to God for his kindness towards us. On that sunny afternoon at Wembley as we sang the Cup Final hymn, *Abide with Me,* I turned and looked at Ian and as we sang our hearts out "In Life, in Death, O Lord, Abide with Me". The tears ran down my face as we turned to each other and embraced in a tight hug.

There is another game which stands out for me during John Gregory's time of managing the club. It was a December game at home to Arsenal and again I was with Ian. We were sat in our then, usual seat in the lower tier of the Holte End.

At half time, Villa were 2-0 down to a rampant Arsenal team and, in truth, being totally outclassed. At half time members of the RAF were treating us to a series of parachute jumps, the last of which was to be 'Father Christmas', who was due to land in the centre circle. All eyes were fixed on the sky and the spectacle that was before us.

Eventually we all (well except for me of course) caught sight of Santa and excitedly 40,000 people watched his descent. As Santa came closer, however, Ian commented that Father Christmas seemed to be heading straight for the roof of the Trinity Road Stand. Within seconds the large crowd gave a collective gasp of horror as they saw

Father Christmas hit the roof and come tumbling to the ground, coming to rest at the side of the pitch. Within a matter of moments, the paramedics and security folk were on hand to administer First Aid. Apparently, there was blood everywhere and a stretcher was brought to carry our mysterious Santa Claus off to hospital. I know the sight of Santa hitting that roof and falling down left a sickening feeling in many people's stomachs and for Ian, I know it was a vivid memory he will never forget. I just have no idea how it affected some of the children who witnessed the horrific scene.

It turned out that the Santa in question, was actually a highly-experienced sky diver by the name of Nigel Rogoff and though he suffered the trauma of having one of his legs amputated, he was in fact lucky to be still alive, having lost litres of blood. I wrote to Nigel to offer him some words of encouragement and consolation. He has gone on to marry one of the nurses who cared for him and it was reported they subsequently became parents of twins. Nigel also continued to raise a great deal of money for charity with some further daring exploits.

After an extensive delay the second half got under way and John Gregory made an astute substitution. Stan Collymore came off the bench to inspire a second half performance by the Villa boys of gargantuan proportions. Collymore played that second half with a great deal of pride in the shirt and his powerful runs into the Gunners' penalty area really got the Villa Park faithful roused and fully behind their team. By the end of the match the game had been turned on its head with Aston Villa coming out as 3-2 winners and apart from Collymore, for whom this was probably his finest display in a Villa shirt, there were also outstanding contributions from all over the field. A real team effort in fact.

At one point during John Gregory's reign Villa were actually top of the Premier League going into the Christmas programme and it was widely reported that during the transfer window John wanted to add Leicester City's Turkish International midfielder, Muzzy Izzet to his squad. The story goes, however, that Doug Ellis refused to sanction the move. Villa eventually petered out that season to finish sixth in the table. Surprisingly, at least from a fan's perspective, John Gregory resigned midway through the following season in January 2002, saying what some departing players had already said – that the Board lacked ambition. This led to a series of fan protests against Doug Ellis. These demonstrations were further fuelled by the written press and some local radio presenters who felt that Doug was taking the club backwards. Mr Ellis, never one to shirk a fight, dug his heels in and appointed another surprise manager.

Graham Taylor, long since removed from the England job, having had loads of abuse heaped upon him by the national press, was invited to take charge for a second time. Taking the reins in February 2002, Taylor stayed for one full season as manager, but regrettably, this did not work out anywhere near as well as it did first time around, adding strength to the adage that you can never go back. Graham became the third manager in a short space of time to resign his position, departing at the end of a season in which Villa finished 16th.

You may recall that I have previously eulogised about Graham Taylor's prowess in the transfer market and even though his stay at Villa Park this time around was short-lived, there was time for him to find another gem. Peter Crouch, the 6ft 7ins striker was signed from Portsmouth for £5m. Many people said this was a waste of money and what on earth did Graham see in this guy to make him want to pay out that kind of money. Crouch has gone on to perform notably for a host of clubs generally and for England in particular.

Villa sadly missed out on Crouch for they sold him on to Southampton for only £2m, whereas later in his career he was commanding fees in the region of £10m.

While in the midst of writing this book, the world of football has been stunned by the announcement of the sudden death of Graham Taylor from a suspected heart attack. Literally hundreds, maybe thousands of tributes have been paid to this extraordinary man for his ability as a coach and a manager, but even more so for his character as a thoroughly decent human being. So many people have testified to the fact that he was extremely kind and would always go the proverbial extra mile to help. My prayers go out in particular to his wife Rita and family. I will say more about Graham later, but for now just to say from me, a fond farewell to the legend that is Graham Taylor.

Former Arsenal defender David O'Leary, who had been out of work since leaving as Leeds United's manager came in as one of the big names, people were clamouring for. Unfortunately, from the outset, David alienated some of the Villa fans by his ill-advised comments relating to the history of the club and the subsequent unrealistic expectations of the supporters. In all of his interviews David O'Leary appeared to be putting down the club and its supporters and he never left you with a feeling of pride about being an Aston Villa supporter. The general consensus was that if he made the supporters feel depressed, what was he doing with the players? He continually made reference to the fact that he had taken over a team in the bottom six of the Premier League and it was going to take a lot of hard work and money to get Villa back into the top half of the table. While it was true that in Graham Taylor's second stint, we had slumped to the lower reaches of the table, in the previous four or five seasons, with basically the same group of players we had always finished top six. Many fans, myself included, felt that the nucleus of the side was good enough to finish well up the league.

While David O'Leary was manager Villa did turn in some reasonable performances and we did get back to being a top half of the table Premier League side. The trouble was that more and more money was going to the top four teams Manchester United, Manchester City, Arsenal and Chelsea. This led to them establishing something of a monopoly when it came to winning trophies.

Eventually the patience of the Board ran out with David O'Leary and his contract was terminated after three fairly uneventful seasons. (The Irishman became known to many as David 'O'Dreary' because of the many boring matches they had to endure at that time). I rate Gavin McCann as one of David O'Leary's best acquisitions for us. McCann turned in many wholehearted, never-say-die displays in the Villa midfield and those attributes always endear players to the home fans.

Chapter 9 - The Revolution

Following the departure of David O'Leary rumours were rife of a takeover at Villa Park. Doug Ellis had been subjected to a series of fan protests over the years, but these had gathered pace since the turn of the century as supporters became increasingly impatient at the lack of silverware being won by the Club. Doug, in my opinion had been a good chairman and a fitting custodian for such a great and prestigious football club as Aston Villa. Just as Aston Villa had been one of the founder members of the Football League back in the 19th century, so now we were also one of the founder members of the Premier League.

We had never been out of that top division under Mr Ellis's reign and I think that in terms of points, Villa were once again in the top six. In that respect, therefore, taking into account our resources compared with other clubs, I do not feel that I, as a supporter, have anything to complain about. I think we have been punching at, or just above our weight over the past 20 years or so. In that regard and many more besides, I think Doug Ellis did an excellent job for Aston Villa and he left us in a very sound financial position, which is more than can be said for the club that he actually inherited back in 1967.

Doug Ellis loved being the top man at Villa Park. He was very proud of the club and proud of his staff and I know he finds it difficult now, not being so involved. May I just pause, to say, thank you Sir Doug Ellis for all you have done for Aston Villa – not perfect of course, but then who is? Time will tell, but I believe that in selling the club to Randy Lerner, Doug made a wise choice for the long term good of Aston Villa Football Club. It would seem that Randy Lerner had a good awareness of the traditions and history of Aston Villa as he worked hard to respect, preserve and build on those excellent qualities. In those early days under the new custodian there was an incredible feel-good factor at the Club. I remember at one game against Sheffield United, everyone who attended at Villa Park, was given a Villa scarf, which bore the slogan 'Proud History – Bright Future', which I loved. Randy Lerner also made the astute observation regarding the British form of what the Americans call 'soccer' that in the UK it would appear that a spiritual bond develops between father and son as they attend games together. Now of course I know you could widen these parent bonding moments to include mothers and daughters, but traditionally, Randy had it right. My Dad and I certainly developed a deep bond as a result of spending so much time together attending Aston Villa matches. They are some of my most cherished memories with my father.

Martin O'Neill was appointed by Doug Ellis just a couple of weeks or so before Randy Lerner's takeover was complete. Some cynics say the best thing Doug Ellis did for Villa was that before selling out he appointed O'Neill. It seems as if O'Neill was a universally popular appointment and certainly Randy Lerner endorsed Martin as one of the best and most intelligent managers in the game. The new broom certainly swept clean as it were and brought new optimism right through the club. Season ticket sales went through the roof and attendances increased season on season. The team's points tally improved in each of the four seasons under the O'Neill regime. You can't knock it, or can you?

When Martin O'Neill walked into the club he had Messiah-like status and it seemed as if, with fans and media alike, he could do no wrong. The club's league position stabilised so we finished in the top six in the final three years of Martin O'Neill's reign. Martin did, however, spend a lot of money bringing in some very good players on high wages. The downside was that Martin also brought in a lot of fringe players, for equally huge fees and big salaries. Martin would frequently remind the media that he did not have a big squad of players, but the opinion of some was that he did not fully utilise the squad he had at his disposal. Off the top of my head now I can think of Steve Sidwell, Marlon Harewood and Habib Beye. There were quite a few others too as the records will show. In addition, Martin failed to give opportunities to some of our very promising young players and he let the likes of Gary Cahill, Steven Davis and Craig Gardner leave after we had invested many years in their development as players.

In the manager's defence, we did also see some exciting attacking football with Ashley Young and Stewart Downing sending in some delicious crosses for the ever-popular John Carew to score. I cannot describe what it takes to acquire legend status at a football club, but Norway International Carew, certainly did that. To hear the song *"John Carew, Carew, he's bigger than me and you, he's gonna score one or two, John Carew, Carew"* reverberate around Villa Park was quite something. It must have made him feel 10 feet tall.

When the world-wide credit crunch came, it would appear to have hit our owner very badly along with what I understand was an expensive divorce settlement. Mr. Lerner continued with the planning of rebuilding the North End stand right up to the end of 2009, although the following spring Paul Faulkner was appointed CEO and major controls on expenditure were implemented. Martin and Randy then had a major falling out, and Martin resigned just five days before the start of the 2010/11 season. This was a crushing hammer blow for the club and its supporters and one from which we have been struggling to recover ever since.

Kevin MacDonald, long time youth and reserve team coach, was thrust into the limelight as caretaker manager for the first few games and many supporters felt he should have been given the job on a permanent basis, so good was his work with the younger players. It was not to be, however and Gerard Houllier, the scholarly Frenchman and former Liverpool manager was appointed. Opinion was divided on this and it certainly took Mr Houllier a while to get his views and playing style across to the players. As a result, we struggled for much of the season in the lower reaches of the table. Three quarters of the way through the campaign Gerard was taken ill and it transpired that he was suffering from a recurrence of the heart problems which had plagued him while he was at Liverpool. In the meantime, assistant manager Gary McAllister took the reins until the end of the season and during that spell in fact results picked up and we finished in a comfortable mid-table position.

After January, our form had improved because the manager had gone out and splashed out a cool £18m to sign England striker Darren Bent from Sunderland. It was Bent's goals which did more than anything else at that time to ensure our top-flight safety.

As that 2010/11 season drew to a close we waited with bated breath to hear what the news about Gerard Houllier's health would be. In the end, on doctor's advice, he decided to resign and step out of high-pressure management altogether. If Gerard Houllier's appointment split opinion down the middle, the next one most certainly did not. Former Scotland player and manager Alex McLeish was installed on a three-year contract. Alex had been manager of our arch rivals Birmingham City for a few years. In that time, he had managed to get them promoted, relegated and won them their first ever major trophy with a League Cup win over Arsenal at Wembley.

The appointment of Alex created a storm of anger and protests that raged in the media throughout his tenure. In my opinion Alex was never given a fair chance to succeed at Villa because of the poisonous atmosphere created at Villa Park by all of the hatred towards him, simply because he had managed the team a few miles down the road. That season Villa were no worse and no better than under Gerrard Houllier. Again, we struggled to stave off relegation and the bill of fare on offer, for the most part was pretty boring. I cannot help but wonder, how much better we might have done had the supporters got behind the Scotsman and created a more positive atmosphere.

Having said all of this, I have to say that the appointment of Alex McLeish showed a naivety on the part of the owner that was surprising to say the least. I would add that the fact Alex took the job too was a surprise to me. After all, he would have known from his days in Scotland the rivalry that exists between Celtic and Rangers, which means I guess, it would be very unusual for someone to go and manage at both clubs without getting a lot of abuse for it. Let me add once more that I do not agree with that kind of behaviour. This is still a sport, not a war and I for one, would always champion the sporting aspects of our 'beautiful' game.

Predictably, Alex lasted just one season. Villa's final match that season was against Norwich City at Carrow Road. We were abysmal and the travelling Villa supporters chanted "You're going to be sacked in the morning". They also chanted "Lambert for Villa". The Norwich City boss, another Scotsman, was the almost universal choice of the Villa fans to be our next manager. It was no surprise when news came through that Alex McLeish had been sacked and I felt really sorry for him and the way he had been treated for simply doing his job. His only crime was that he had managed Birmingham City. I was impressed by the way in which Alex conducted himself with such a high level of integrity and decorum.

So it was, that the great majority of Villa supporters had their way. The former Birmingham City boss was ousted and Paul Lambert arrived at Villa Park on a tidal wave of positivity. This was to herald a brand-new dawn for Aston Villa, but regrettably, yet again, it was not to be. In fairness, Paul Lambert had done a good job in his previous management roles and as a player he had achieved much, playing for Celtic and Scotland with great distinction. His crowning glory was to win the European Champions League with the German side Borussia Dortmund.

From the outset, however, his time at Villa was a struggle and in his first season we suffered a heavy 8-0 drubbing at Chelsea, followed by conceding a further seven goals in the next two games. Aston Villa were starting to have a reputation as a boring team with very few shots on goal. We did rally a bit towards the end of Paul's first season and finished just below mid-table after struggling in the bottom six for the most part.

In the second season, boring was again the watchword and we struggled to score many goals and suffered more home defeats than at any other time in Villa's history. People were already beginning to question whether Paul Lambert should be sacked and we survived being relegated by a couple of points. For the very first time in my life as a Villa supporter I felt it would be right to have a change of manager; someone was needed with a more positive and upbeat approach. Yet the hierarchy stood by Paul Lambert, and the start of his third season in charge was a bit more encouraging. Somehow, we managed to secure ten points from the first four games and that was enough, for some strange reason, to secure the manager a new four-year contract. Just maybe, the powers-that-be knew something we as supporters did not. Unfortunately, it was not to be, because we then went on a disastrous run that led to us picking up only two wins in the next 24 games, leaving us in the bottom two of the Premier League.

Aston Villa had become a laughing stock and we held many unwanted records. The latest of these was that we had scored less goals than any other top flight team in the whole of Europe. It really was desperate. Of the many players that Paul Lambert had brought in, admittedly on drastically reduced wages compared to the Martin O'Neill era, it was hard to think of a real success. There is no doubt in my mind that Belgium International hotshot Christian Benteke would take the accolade. He was a talismanic striker, whose often-spectacular goals did most to keep Villa in the Premier League over that dismal three-year period. Dutchman Ron Vlaar, when fit, was a good leader and skipper during a difficult period of the Club's history. Lastly, I would include goalkeeper Brad Guzan in that list because when Paul Lambert took over, Brad was out of contract and had gone back to the United States. Villa caught up with Brad on their pre-season tour and having watched him in training, the manager decided to offer him a new contract at Villa Park. It was a great piece of business on the part of our new manager.

Meanwhile the season dragged on relentlessly with Villa falling ever closer to the trap door, and after what was described widely in the media as a gutless performance against fellow relegation candidates Hull City, which we lost 2-0, the axe eventually fell and Paul Lambert was dismissed. Never in my 60 years as an Aston Villa supporter had I wanted a manager to lose his job. I had absolutely nothing personal against Paul Lambert, but things had to change and quickly if Villa were going to preserve their Premier League status. Personally, I along with many other devoted supporters, felt that we were odds on to be relegated to the Championship, but something bordering on a football miracle was about to unfold.

Rookie manager Tim Sherwood was brought in by Villa's recently appointed CEO Tom Fox, who had come in from Arsenal replacing the outgoing Paul Faulkner. Tim Sherwood had been out of work since leaving Tottenham Hotspur, for whom he had been acting manager in the final dozen or so games of the previous season. Tim had gained a reputation of being a fine coach of young players and for playing an attractive style of football. He also knew what it was to be a winner as he had captained Blackburn Rovers to the Premier League title back in the 1990s. Tim's reign in the Villa Park hot seat began quietly with two narrow home defeats to Stoke City and Swansea City. Both performances were much improved however and we only lost points due to a couple of individual errors. We did make progress in the FA Cup though and a resounding 4-0 triumph against Sunderland at the Stadium of Light gave everyone a lift and the belief that just maybe we could escape the drop.

Shortly afterwards an amazing few days took place in the life of this great club. We beat our local rivals West Bromwich Albion under the Villa Park lights 2-1, with a last-minute Christian Benteke goal that moved us out of the relegation zone in what was a spine-tingling atmosphere, the likes of which I had not experienced for many years. Four days later we beat them again for the second time at Villa Park in the 6th round of the FA Cup. This time it was 2-0 and would you believe it, we were now through to a semi-final appearance at the new Wembley Stadium. It later transpired, once the round had been completed that we would play the mighty (or should that be once-mighty?) Liverpool.

Tim Sherwood had transformed this group of players into a side that were now playing an attacking and exciting brand of football. My brother Paul, for instance, emailed me to say that he woke up every morning with excitement inside him and he could not wait for the next game. A far cry from what we had been suffering for two or three years before. I remember emailing Tom Fox to thank him for making the switch and congratulating him on the appointment of Tim Sherwood. After a few more games, where we picked up some vital points, it was time to prepare for the semi-final clash at Wembley. Again, I travelled to London with Ian, more in hope than expectation. This after all was a bonus after the misery of what had gone before.

It felt strange being at Wembley for something other than a Cup Final, but nevertheless it was pretty special and even more so because of what took place on the hallowed turf. The Villa players turned in a magnificent performance to defeat Liverpool by two goals to one after going behind in the first half. Goals from Christian Benteke and skipper Fabian Delph saw Villa through to their first FA Cup Final in 15 years.

The atmosphere at the game was incredible and the Villa supporters made a fantastic noise, out-singing their illustrious counterparts from Liverpool. It was magical that Tim Sherwood had turned the club's fortunes around in such spectacular fashion. Taking nothing for granted though, there was still Premier League safety to be achieved and this was done courtesy of two victories at Villa Park against Everton and West Ham United. That was a welcome upturn in fortunes for the home fans, who over the previous few seasons had witnessed precious few victories. These two wins were priceless, however and even though the lads suffered a humiliating 6-1 drubbing at Southampton in the penultimate game of the season, the fact that Hull City lost 2-0 to Tottenham meant that Villa's top flight status was secure for another season.

Mission accomplished, therefore, for the ebullient Tim Sherwood. Now it was time to fully focus on the end of season finale, the showpiece FA Cup Final against Arsenal; the team who had already given Villa two footballing lessons that season, winning 3-0 at Villa Park and 5-0 at the Emirates Stadium. This was a one-off occasion though when, because of nerves, anything can happen. The dreamers among us wondered, could the Aston Villa team of 2015 actually go and win the FA Cup for the first time since those Peter McParland heroics some 58 years earlier.

Well the short answer is no, and what a resounding no it was! On the day, Arsenal were magnificent and at times mesmerising with their flowing football. Arsenal, in this form, as much as any other team in the world, epitomise the phrase 'the beautiful game'. They outplayed Villa from start to finish and the Villa boys never once got into their stride. We never had a shot in the whole game or even a corner. It was as though the ghost of Paul Lambert had returned to haunt us. Apart from goalkeeper Shay Given, no other player did himself justice and we succumbed tamely to a 4-0 defeat with people saying it was the most one-sided Cup Final they could ever remember. Yet another humiliation. It was a great shame really because since the arrival of Tim Sherwood, the team as a whole had played well and individuals such as Christian Benteke, Fabian Delph and the new rising star, Jack Grealish, had been sensational.

The day of the Cup Final and the week leading up to it had been pretty special for me, though. Firstly, having swapped many an email with Villa CEO Tom Fox, I was invited to Villa Park to meet him, to be shown around the ground and to have some photographs taken. Having been notified of my great love for Aston Villa over many years, an ITV cameraman turned up on the day to film me at home and at Villa Park. The footage went out on the local Central News that night. The cameras were back at my house on the Friday morning and this time I went out nationally on the late-night ITV news. I even received emails from people on holiday in the Canary Islands, to say they had seen me on the news.

The excitement did not stop there because it had been arranged for me to meet my all-time Aston Villa hero, Peter McParland, at

Wembley the following day. My son, Ian and I met up with Peter for a long chat and photographs at Starbucks, just outside Wembley Stadium. Peter, now 81, was in good form and we chatted non-stop as I reminded him of games and goals I had seen way back in the 1950s and 1960s. It was great fun meeting such a legend and I was so impressed with Peter's knowledge and insights into the modern game. Again, these pictures were shown on ITV in the following days. Throughout the next two weeks I had people coming up to me in the street and on the bus to say they had seen me on the television. Quite a few wanted to chat about football and players from the old days. These things will live in my memory for ever and have already helped ease the pain of that Cup Final humiliation.

Little did I know that the shame of the manner of that Cup Final defeat, was only the forerunner to even greater heartache and embarrassment that lay just around the corner.

Chapter 10 - The Trap Door Opens

Tim Sherwood performed a minor miracle in guiding Aston Villa to Premier League safety at the back end of the 2015/16 season. The two wins against West Bromwich Albion in the same week – one in the league and one in the FA Cup – gave everyone a massive lift. Then to go to Wembley twice in the matter of weeks was more than we Villa supporters dared dream of. As stated earlier, the win against all the odds in the FA Cup semi-final will always be one of my most treasured memories. It truly was as brilliant as it was surprising.

It was at this time that I began to have a growing conviction I should seek to reintroduce a prayer group to get behind Aston Villa and reconnect it in some way with its Christian roots. I spoke with a couple of Villa fans in my local church and they agreed it would be good to meet up to pray. We decided to meet on the first Saturday of each month from 9am to 9.45am to pray about everything and everyone concerned with the Club. Little did we know that the forthcoming season was going to be one of the most disastrous in the long history of Aston Villa Football Club. God knew, however and one of the things I have discovered through reading the Bible and in my own experience, is that things often get worse before they get better. To this day, Geoff Kyte, Mark Leonard and myself are still faithfully meeting each month to pray for the Club we love. If you want to join us then just be in touch by email and I will give further details.

After the Cup Final capitulation, Tim Sherwood made it clear that there would need to be wholesale changes before the start of the new season. Sadly for us, the four most important players in the team all left. Influential Dutch centre back Ron Vlaar chose not to accept a new contract, Tom Cleverley (on loan from Manchester

United) signed for Everton, and leading goal scorer and talisman Christian Benteke went to Liverpool for a huge fee. The biggest kick in the teeth of all was skipper Fabian Delph leaving for Manchester City having, only a few days before, pledged his future to Aston Villa.

In a short space of time a large number of new players were brought in and Tim Sherwood had the difficult task of welding them into a team ready for the opening day encounter away at newly promoted Bournemouth. Not a bad start though, for apart from being under the cosh for most of the match, we came away with a 1-0 victory thanks to a goal from new signing Rudy Gestede. Was this to be the start of an exciting new era? Unfortunately not, because after 10 games that was our solitary victory and we were lying perilously close to the bottom of the table. In fairness to Tim Sherwood and his team, all of our defeats had been by the odd goal and no team had actually outplayed us. It was taking more time than we expected for the new players to blend in with the older ones and individual errors were costing us dear. The pressure was mounting on Tim Sherwood though and, prematurely in my opinion, the axe fell once again and our manager had gone after less than six months in the job.

A few weeks later, former Arsenal player Remi Garde was appointed and charged with the task of reviving our ailing season. By this time, we had imported quite a few French-speaking players and it was thought that Remi, along with his French-speaking assistant Eric Black, would be able to get more out of the team as a whole.

The new manager was appointed by my good friend, CEO Tom Fox, but I have to say, it was one that seemed doomed to failure from the start. Throughout the entire season (and it pains me to say it) Aston Villa only won two more games, those being against Crystal Palace and Norwich City, both at Villa Park. We finished bottom of the table with only 17 points and a long way adrift of the other relegated Clubs, Newcastle United and Norwich City. The season was marred by bouts of ill-discipline on and off the field by certain experienced players, who should have known better. Many fans turned against certain players and there was growing unrest against the owner Randy Lerner and many of his staff. Fuelled by endless local and national radio phone in programmes and newspaper polls, the mood grew ever more toxic. Villa Park was not a nice place to be on match days. Our relegation to the Championship was sealed long before the end of the season and so waiting for the end to come was like going through a long, lingering death. Randy Lerner had been trying to sell the club for about two years, but without success. Relegation, however, seemed to herald an upsurge of interest by potential buyers, possibly at a knock-down price, so maybe, just maybe there would be some light at the end of this very dark tunnel.

Just like Tim Sherwood before him, Remi Garde's stay as Aston Villa manager was a short one and he left the club by mutual consent once relegation had become a mathematical certainty. Relegation was confirmed for the first time in just under 30 years and rumours of potential takeovers began to surface. Randy Lerner appointed businessman Steve Hollis to oversee a cost-cutting exercise and to facilitate any possible takeover. There were lots of internal changes within the club and unfortunately, as happens with relegation, a lot of people were made redundant. Speculation increased day by day, however, that there were several parties genuinely interested in buying the club from Randy Lerner. Eventually news broke and was later confirmed that Aston Villa football club had been bought by the Chinese businessman, Dr Tony Xia. Having done what he was brought in to do, Steve Hollis left with everyone's best wishes. Dr Tony was introduced to the Press and immediately began to say all of the right things about making Aston Villa one of the greatest clubs in the world. He indicated that he would base himself in the West Midlands for at least a year and be very hands on in terms of developing things at Villa Park and also at the training ground.

Roberto Di Matteo, who ironically scored the only goal in Chelsea's 1-0 victory over us in the 2000 FA Cup Final, was brought in as our new manager in June 2016, with Steve Clarke as his assistant. It was hoped that the new duo would return the club to the Premier League, however Di Matteo had a disastrous run winning only one of the 11 Championship games during his reign and he lost his job after just 124 days. It was a shame really, because, a bit like Tim Sherwood one year earlier, we had actually played some nice football, often only failing to win because of individual errors and conceding late goals. As is often said, the difference between success and failure is often down to fine margins.

In October 2016, Dr Tony replaced Di Matteo with Steve Bruce, an experienced manager who came from Hull City after successfully guiding them to the Premier League. Some 10 years or so earlier, Steve did of course manage Birmingham City, but his arrival did not meet with anything like that of Alex McLeish a few years before.

Personally, I have always liked Steve Bruce as a manager and someone who is well respected within the game. He also comes across as a fine man, which is important to me. I truly believe that given the time and tools to succeed, he is the right man to guide Aston Villa back to the very top. I believe Randy Lerner was right when he issued those scarves and that for Aston Villa supporters we can declare 'Proud History Bright Future' in the capable hands of our new owner Dr Tony Xia. I love the vision outlined by Dr Tony to make Aston Villa Football clubs one of the very top and most successful teams in the world. I am sure all we Villa supporters say a very loud "Amen" to that.

Chapter 11 - Words of Encouragement

Being trained as a typist after going blind as a teenager was a big blow to my male ego, and I go in to this in much more detail in my autobiographical book *Fear, Fun and Faith,* but with hindsight it has turned out to be highly providential. It has been great to sit at a keyboard; initially a manual typewriter, then the electric variety and now the computer, to be able to type my letters and articles at a reasonably fast pace. That, together with becoming a Christian has put me in the perfect place to write to people with a fair degree of understanding and compassion. Over the years, I have written to hundreds of people – the famous and the not so famous alike.

Since personally experiencing God's love at the age of 21, I have had a desire to share that love with others. That has motivated me to write to many folk, who are going through tough times, in order to offer them some words of encouragement. I may hear about someone on the radio, or in a newspaper article and God will put that person on my heart, or in my thoughts and I know I must write offering some words of consolation and support.

I have written to royalty, sportsmen and women, politicians and pop stars and had many interesting replies from the likes of Tommy Steele, Boney M, John Major and even members of the Royal family. With regard to footballers I have usually written when they are facing long term and often career-threatening injuries. I feel that I can relate to them in that my football playing days were cut cruelly short at the age of 19. Even though I was not playing football for a living, nevertheless, it was my passion and I do not think anyone could have loved playing the game more than me. I therefore felt the disappointment and sense of loss as much as anyone else whether they be professional or not. I have been able to write therefore from a position of empathy and also to say, great though football is, I have, in Jesus, found someone who is far more wonderful and that faith in him is totally satisfying. Through a personal faith in Jesus it is absolutely possible to live a fulfilled life whether we have plenty or whether we have barely enough. It's all about connecting to the source and discovering our destiny through that relationship.

One of the first people I can remember writing to was Steve Coppell when he was an outstanding winger for Manchester United. Steve had suffered an horrendous injury – I think a badly broken leg, which was threatening to end his great career. I was thrilled to get a really nice letter back from Steve and in part of that letter, apart from thanking me for writing and saying what an encouragement my letter had been, he said that he wished he had the faith which I had.

While on the subject of Manchester United, I once wrote to George Best. George had been the subject of a television documentary which I had watched and it gave a glimpse into the kind of pressure George was living under at the height of his popularity, not just as a footballer, but as a personality in the late sixties and early seventies. Of course, the initiated will know that George Best was treated in many ways like the Beatles and some even said he was like the fifth Beatle.

In the documentary, it was revealed one of George's sisters was a Christian and she said that George carried his Mum's Bible with him everywhere he went. In my letter to George, which was highly complimentary of his skills, I also encouraged him to actually read that Bible afresh as I felt it could bring him wisdom and guidance as it had done for me. Fearing that George might not get my letter I sent it via the team manager at the time, Frank O'Farrell. I was thrilled to get a letter back from Frank saying he appreciated me writing to George and he said that if George had true friends like me, then he would not be in half the trouble that he was. It was a really nice letter and though I never heard from George, I was heartened by Frank O'Farrell's reply and his promise to pass my letter on. In fact, George's non-response was an early indicator to me that I would not get that many replies percentage-wise from footballers in the future. It's a strange thing to me that I can write to footballers and receive very few responses, whereas when I write to managers, they nearly all reply. Funny thing is, they too were footballers once. I guess they must have had some PR or courtesy training along the way.

In the 1980s I went through an interesting phase, where having written, I received a hat-trick of responses by telephone. The first one was from Aston Villa's Championship and European Cup-winning centre half Allan Evans. I cannot even recall exactly what I wrote to him about now, but one teatime when we were sat down as a family, the phone began to ring. One of my daughters answered and came back saying, "It's for you Dad, someone named Allan Evans wants to speak with you".

Somewhat shocked, I got up from the table to take the call. It was great to hear Allan's rich Scottish brogue on the end of the line. He told me that he and his wife had read my letter in bed the night before and they had found it really touching. He also said that it had greatly encouraged him at a difficult time in his career.

Shortly after that my family and I moved to Cornwall to live in Redruth as I was about to commence a training course at Harvest Bible College. Of course, I was going to the one part of England where there was no professional football league team so that was going to be hard. Cornwall, of course, is primarily a Rugby Union county, but in terms of professional football, BBC Radio Cornwall, did cover the Devon clubs Exeter City, Torquay United and Plymouth Argyle.

One day I was listening to an interview with the then Plymouth manager Dave Smith – yet another Scotsman. I was really impressed and I have to say quite inspired by this interview and it turned out that Dave Smith used to post positive sayings on the team dressing room walls. The interviewer asked Dave to give an example of some of these and about 50% of the ones he read out were in fact straight from the Bible. Some of the phrases included were:

I can do all things through Christ who strengthens me.

If you have faith the size of a mustard seed, you can move mountains.

All things are possible to those who believe.

And there were many more besides. I decided therefore to write to Dave and to tell him something of my story. A few days later, I answered the phone when it rang in our kitchen only to be greeted with the words, "Hi John, this is Dave Smith from Plymouth Argyle". Dave thanked me for my letter and for my inspiring story and all in all we had about 15 minutes on the phone, during which time he told me of his time being brought up in the Boy's Brigade and learning some of those Bible verses. Dave and I became quite good friends for a while and later that season he invited me, along with my son and some friends, to be guests of the club when Plymouth Argyle played Aston Villa. It was a good afternoon all round. We got to meet the Plymouth players before the game, but disappointingly not the Villa players. That minor setback was more than offset however, as Villa won the game 3-1 with two goals coming from Mark Walters.

The third phone call came from Villa midfielder Andy Blair who I had written to following another radio interview I had heard. Andy was a delightful and easy man to chat with and he again expressed his deep appreciation for my letter, which had brought him so much encouragement.

I also took time to write to Kevin Gage, a hardworking right full back and occasional midfield player who was bought by Graham Taylor from Wimbledon. Kevin formed a more than useful full back pairing with Stuart Gray at the time. Kevin did, however, at one point suffer a loss of form and as happens with some players, the home supporters got on his back, jeering and booing when he got the ball. That kind of treatment of players quite honestly sickens me and I really felt for Kevin, who was as honest a player as you would ever see. I wrote with some words which I hoped would lift the man's spirit and raise his confidence levels and he wrote me the most wonderful letter back, detailing how he had been feeling, but saying that my words had given him fresh hope. That meant a great deal to me.

Even the genius and enigmatic Brian Clough received a letter from me once. The older ones reading these recollections may remember that Brian conducted a one-man campaign to try and clean up the obscene chanting that was coming from the terraces. At the one end of the City Ground in Nottingham, where Clough was manager at the time, he had a sign erected which said, 'No Swearing Please, Brian', which I thought was pretty impressive, if totally unrealistic. Brian's wish to make football grounds and certainly the one at Nottingham Forest, more family friendly, was highly commendable.

During the time of that one-man campaign, I heard Brian Clough being interviewed on a Midlands television news feature and in light of his clean up mission, I could hardly believe my ears, as I heard

Brian swear twice in a three-minute interview. Did the roguish Mr Clough do that on purpose I wonder, or was he just so passionate about this subject that his lips just ran away with him? Whatever the reason, I did not miss out on the opportunity to write and applaud the man for his laudable campaign, but gently suggested he should lead by example. I have to admit I half dreaded any reply. I need not have worried, however, for even though the reply was brief – two sentences in all – Brian did apologise for his double slip of the tongue.

One man I do wish to honour for the quality and depth of his letters is Graham Taylor. Whenever I have written to him, which over the years has been four or five times, he has always given me the courtesy of an extremely well-written and thoughtful response, even to the point of being chatty and talking about his family and walking with his dog in the park. I call that treating people with respect and if only more people did that today what a nicer world this would be.

I will conclude this section by telling you about Willie Bell, the former Leeds United, Leicester City and Scottish International left back. When I wrote to Willie he was manager of Birmingham City. I was living in Market Harborough, Leicestershire at the time and with my radio aerial stuck out of the bathroom window I was listening to a radio phone in on BRMB in Birmingham. That was the only place in the house where I could get decent reception. I lay in the bath therefore and listened transfixed as Willie Bell in the studio fielded calls from angry Birmingham City supporters, who were disgruntled at the Blues run of poor form, tactics and team selection. I was amazed and inspired at the gracious way Willie dealt with many of these aggressive and often downright rude callers.

At the end of the one-hour programme, the presenter thanked Willie for being there and made a comment along the lines of "I bet you feel you've been beaten black and blue, don't you?", to which Willie just replied "It's all part of the job and the fans have a right to complain".

When the programme had finished I quickly got out of the bath, dried myself down and went to my typewriter. Of course, I wrote to Willie and thanked him for his impeccable manners and great grace in the way in which he spoke to people who were hostile towards him. I said it reminded me of a verse from the Bible which says, 'A gentle answer turned away anger'. I went on to say to Willie that I did not know if he was a Christian or not, but he had perfectly demonstrated to me as a Christian the virtue of humility. I went on to say that I would pray for him on a daily basis for the following two months. I don't normally say things quite so specific, but on that occasion, I felt really impressed by God to say that and to make that commitment. I posted my letter on the Saturday morning and that afternoon I think Birmingham lost 4-0 at home to Liverpool. On the day my letter arrived on Willie Bell's desk he actually got the sack. So much for my letter and so much for my prayers, I thought to myself. I really thought that would be the end of it.

A couple of months later I received a postcard from the USA and it was from Willie and Mary Bell. I could hardly believe it as my wife read it out to me. Willie apologised for not replying to my letter, but said what a great encouragement it was to him and to his family. After losing his job at Birmingham City he had gone out with Mary to America to see some friends, who had invited them to a church meeting they were attending. It was during that time that Willie and Mary had made a decision to become committed Christians. In Willie's card he wrote that my letter had been the start of the process, which had led to them making the most important decision of their lives. What an enormous thrill that was for me and so encouraging for my faith too.

A short while afterwards the Bell family came back to the UK and Willie was appointed manager of Lincoln City. While he was there Sylvia and I went to stay with them in their home for a weekend and I also had the honour of being invited to preach at the local church Willie and Mary were attending at the time. Later after ceasing to be manager at Lincoln City, Willie went back to live in the States where he became a football coach to boys at Liberty Bible School in Virginia. Willie would then take teams out across the United States and other countries to coach in schools and share their faith with the schoolchildren.

I have lost touch with the family now, but I understand they are back in the UK and have a ministry to prisoners and ex-offenders in the north of England. Letter writing has taken a bit of a back seat for me in recent years as emails and writing my first two books have taken precedence. This little sequence, however, has reinvigorated and convinced me that there are plenty of people out there in the big wide world who could do with some unexpected words of encouragement so why don't you try it too!

Chapter 12 - The Times They Are A Changing

People like me, who were teenagers in the 1960s, usually look back on those days with a lovely warm glow and a feeling of how great and momentous that era was. Of course, we are looking through rose-coloured spectacles, as the saying goes, because enjoyable though they were, a lot of things took place at that time, which were not so good. Indeed, I feel that many of the things which are bad about our society today are the results of seeds which were sown in the sixties or even late fifties. Music, movies and by and large sport were really great in those days, reflecting the message of freedom that was coming at us from all angles. I won't comment further on that here as this is not a sociological book, but all I want to say is that in the sixties things began to change in all walks of life. Bob Dylan was proved to be right in his song *The Times They Are A Changing'* and football was not exempt from this revolution.

I think it began to happen as a result of Alf Ramsey's England winning the World Cup in 1966 with his team of 'Wingless Wonders' as they were called. For over 100 years before that, a football team consisted of a goalkeeper, right back, left back, right half, centre half, left half, right winger (or outside right), inside right, centre forward, inside left and a left winger (or outside left), with no hint of a substitute. Sir Alf's team, however, was in a 4-4-2 formation, or was it 4-3-3? Overlapping full backs came in, as did centre backs, midfield players and strikers. This revolution was to steadily continue until we have what we have today where numbers on shirts mean nothing other than the fact that they are a marketing tool for the club and its shirt sponsor.

Before change kicked in, there was a degree of stability and constancy which was both reassuring and comforting. This is true of course right across society and not just in football, but here I am deliberately only concentrating on the football aspect. Nowadays it would be hard even for the most enthusiastic fan to reel off the name of its team's first XI as football has become such a squad game and many clubs, even lower down the leagues, operate the rotation system. Back in the fifties and sixties, however, you could quite easily, almost mechanically, trot out the names of most, if not all of a club's first XI. Let me have a go now off the cuff as it were...

Birmingham City's team that lost to Manchester City in the 1956 FA Cup Final, the one in which the Manchester City goalkeeper, Bert Trautmann was injured and miraculously played on with a broken neck, rolls off my tongue even though I was only 8 years of age at the time. It was Gil Merrick, Jeff Hall (tragically to die from polio a short while later), Ken Green, Len Boyd (captain), Trevor Smith, Roy Warhurst, Gordon Astall, Noel Kinsey, Eddy Brown, Peter Murphy and Alex Govan. Of course, Birmingham City fans are universally known for the song they sing to get behind their team. *Keep Right On to the End of the Road* has become a stirring anthem for the club and it was introduced to them by their Scottish left winger Alex Govan. I do wish Aston Villa had a stirring anthem we could sing like that one! Ironically in 1957 in the run that led up to us winning the FA Cup, we adopted the song "It's a Long Way to Tipperary", slightly adapting the lyric to say "It's a Long Way to go to Wembley" and including the words "Goodbye Bristol city, farewell Middlesbrough". I think it came out after the 5th round and turned out to be prophetic with us going on to win against Manchester United in that never to be forgotten final.

Blackburn Rovers had a pretty memorable side in the early sixties and this one comes to mind pretty easily: Harry Leyland, John Bray, Keith Newton, Ron Clayton (England International and captain), Matt Woods, Mick McGrath, Brian Douglas, Peter Dobing, Derek Dougan, Dave Whelan (former owner of JJB sports and Wigan

120

Athletic FC) and Ally MacLeod (later to become manager of Scotland). The Rovers were a classy footballing side who tore Villa to shreds on more than one occasion.

West Ham United were throughout the 1960s and early 1970s one of the most attractive teams to watch and one particular team stands out for me. I remember them coming to play at Villa Park in their all sky-blue kit with a claret hoop on the shirt. They looked so classy and they played smart with a team that read Lawrie Leslie, John Bond, Noel Cantwell, Eddie Bovington, Ken Brown, Bobby Moore (the classiest wing half I ever saw), Peter Brabrook, Ron Boyce, Johnny Byrne, Geoff Hurst, John Sissons. Notice the numbers of players whose initial began with the letter 'B'. Other players who featured in the Hammers side around that time were John Dick, Jim Standen (the goalkeeper/cricketer I talked about earlier) and Martin Peters. A team full of silky skills if ever there was one.

The brilliant Tottenham Hotspur team of that era too is one never to be forgotten and all these years later even with someone who is not a Spurs fan, the names just roll off the tongue: Bill Brown, Peter Baker, Ron Henry, Danny Blanchflower (captain and ex-Villa player of course), Maurice Norman, Dave Mackay (can there ever have been a tougher tackler in the game?), Terry Medwin, John White (tragically to be killed when struck by lightning), Bobby Smith, Les Allen and Cliff Jones. Terry Dyson and the legendary goal scorer Jimmy Greaves were also later integrated into this team which functioned like a highly-tuned Rolls Royce.

Wolverhampton Wanderers were another team I enjoyed watching and the following players come easily to mind along with their traditional old gold shirts and black shorts: Malcolm Finlayson, Eddie Stuart, Gerry Harris, Eddie Clamp, Billy Wright (legend for both Wolves and England), Ron Flowers, Norman Deeley, Peter

Broadbent, Jim Murray, Colin Booth and Jimmy Mullen. Players such as Bill Slater, Ted Farmer and Alan Hinton would also be added to this team.

Many other teams of that time had seven or eight players who would instantly come to mind so let me jog a few memories by mentioning some of them. The great Busby babes of Manchester United included Roger Byrne, Tommy Taylor, Eddie Colman, Dennis Viollet, David Pegg, Bobby Charlton and the majestic Duncan Edwards. One can only surmise what he may have gone on to achieve in the game. Burnley were another team of stars and silky skills in the 1960s with such outstanding players as Jimmy McIlroy, Ray Pointer, John Connelly, goalkeepers Colin McDonald and Adam Blacklaw and the brilliant full back partnership of John Angus and Alex Elder.

Leeds United had a half back line which again, rolled off the tongue in Bremner, Charlton and Hunter. Did they ever come tougher than that? Reaney and Bell were the full back partnership in that team, while up front you had the likes of Allan Clarke and Mick Jones. Leeds also possessed a very tricky left winger in those days by the name of Albert Johanneson. He was outstanding not just because he was such a fabulous footballer, but because he was one of the few black players in the English game at the time.

The team geographically closest to Aston Villa is of course, not Birmingham City, but West Bromwich Albion and they too have always been synonymous with exciting open football. I grew up watching such stars at The Hawthorns as Don Howe, Bobby Robson, Ronnie Allen (who I always thought bore a remarkable resemblance to the singer Frankie Vaughan) and Derek Kevan. I recall that the Albion for a time had two Welsh International full backs by the name of Williams; Stuart and Graham to be precise.

122

Chapter 13 - Flanner's Favourites

Now allow me to focus on individual positions for a while. Growing up watching football in the fifties and sixties I became aware how many fine goalkeepers there were playing in the English First Division. Some of those I grew to appreciate and enjoy watching are as follows:

Adam Blacklaw – Burnley

Fred Else – Preston North End

George Farm – Blackpool

Harry Gregg – Manchester United

Peter Grummitt – Nottingham Forest

Alan Hodgkinson – Sheffield United

Eddie Hopkinson – Bolton Wanderers

Kevin Keelan – Norwich City

Tommy Lawrence – Liverpool

Lawrie Leslie – West Ham United

Johnny Schofield – Birmingham City

Geoff Sidebottom – Aston Villa

Nigel Sims – Aston Villa

Ron Springett – Sheffield Wednesday

Colin Withers – Aston Villa

Gordon West – Everton

Bert Trautmann - Manchester City

Jack Kelsey - Arsenal

From that far-from comprehensive list you will see that there were some truly great goalkeepers around at the time and I have not even included the most obvious one in Gordon Banks of Leicester City. Now let's have a look at some of the centre forwards I enjoyed watching:

Ronnie Allen – West Bromwich Albion

Johnny Byrne – West Ham United

Derek Dougan – Aston Villa

Ted Farmer – Wolverhampton Wanderers

Tony Hateley – Aston Villa

Gerry Hitchens – Aston Villa

Ray Pointer – Burnley

Bobby Smith – Tottenham Hotspur

Ian St John – Liverpool

There was a time when every team had in its side what we used to call a 'schemer'. This is probably what we now term as a playmaker or a midfield general, someone in fact who could open up defences with a brilliant pass or a piece of dribbling skill that would leave opposing players in his wake. I list below therefore some of my favourite schemers of their day:

Peter Broadbent - Wolverhampton Wanderers

Peter Dobing – Blackburn Rovers

Johnny Giles – Leeds United

Johnny Haynes – Fulham

Bobby Hope – West Bromwich Albion

Jimmy McIlroy – Burnley

Dennis Viollet – Manchester United

John White – Tottenham Hotspur

Phil Woosnam – Aston Villa

Ron Wylie – Aston Villa

How about wingers who excited me and who I loved to watch no matter which side they were on? Some of these you will be able to pre-empt, but here is the list anyway:

Willie Anderson – Aston Villa

Bertie Auld – Birmingham City

John Berry – Manchester United

Harry Burrows – Aston Villa

Ian Callaghan – Liverpool

Clive Clark – West Bromwich Albion

Bryan Douglas – Blackburn Rovers

Tom Finney – Preston North End

Mike Hellawell – Birmingham City

Alan Hinton – Wolverhampton Wanderers

Albert Johanneson – Leeds United

Cliff Jones – Tottenham Hotspur

Stanley Matthews – Blackpool

Peter McParland – Aston Villa

David Pegg – Manchester United

Peter Thompson – Liverpool

I guess there's nothing quite so exciting on a football field as seeing an out-and-out winger running down the flanks, taking on his full back to put in a cross, or cut inside to shoot. I am sure you could add your own particular favourites to the list. For now, I just want to reflect on the fact that football is about the players who play the game, who light up the pitch with their dazzling skills and the goals, saves or tackles that live in the memory for many years to come.

Chapter 14 - Whose Game Is It Anyway?

Kick Off Times

Many decisions that are made surrounding the modern game would appear not to take into account the people who really matter – the supporters. The timing of matches for instance seems to lie almost entirely with the wishes of the television channels who are pumping money into the sport, allied to a few match timings, which are influenced by the local police. It would appear that little or no consideration is given to whether the timing is convenient for the supporters or not. A classic example of this was when Aston Villa were scheduled to play Birmingham City. The kick off was often rearranged for a Sunday at 12 noon, or as has happened once, 11am. This in my opinion is a crazy time as it penalises all kinds of people from getting to the game. Firstly, there are those boys and men who play football for fun on a Sunday morning, of which there are still a great number. Many of those people may have already bought season tickets for example in the hope of supporting their team.

The other people who suffer are the football supporters who still choose, out of conviction and sincere faith, to attend Church. Remembering, as I said earlier, that many football clubs started off from a Church base, this is no way to respect our roots and heritage. In addition, with football matches kicking off at such a time it can spoil things for people on the way to a Church service as they can often get caught up in the crowds and the accompanying traffic congestion. To my mind playing professional football matches on a Sunday morning should be avoided and resisted at all costs.

Ahead of the 2016-17 season, the day and kick off times for Aston Villa v Birmingham City games were switched to Sundays at midday at the request of the West Midlands Police. Once again, peace-loving people who attend Church, or play Sunday League football are being made to pay the price – the drunken hooligans win again! We are masters at treating the symptoms and not getting to the root cause.

Yellow and Red Cards

Throughout a season there is so much controversy surrounding the awarding of yellow and red cards. I believe, as a paying spectator, that all efforts should be made to keep 22 footballers on the field of play. That is what I and other people pay our hard-earned cash to see. Football should be a contest between two teams of 11 players on each side. Some people pay hundreds of pounds out to travel to a match, only to have it ruined either by over-zealous refereeing, or what are, in my opinion, crazy rules invented by football administrators. A sending off should be the ultimate sanction for a dangerous foul or for insulting or abusive behaviour. Two yellow cards should not automatically lead to a sending off, but should go on a player's disciplinary points tally.

The game in question should always have 22 players on the field no matter what. Where a player is legitimately dismissed then I believe a replacement should be allowed off the substitutes bench and count as one of the three substitutes. Increasingly it seems we are getting red cards rescinded the following week once the disciplinary panel have sat. That is good in part, especially for the club and the player, but that does not change the result and it does not appease the supporters, who have been robbed of the competitive match they paid to see.

Prior to losing my sight, I can recall a game when Stan Lynn, Villa's right-back dived to save a shot on the goal line after our goalkeeper had been beaten. The result was a penalty to the opposition. I cannot recall if Stan even had his name taken, as it was in those days. Again, I feel a penalty and a yellow card is sufficient punishment in a case like this. Seeing a full-back dive to punch the ball away was not in my day seen as cheating, but all good fun and part of the day's entertainment. Now it has all become so serious and lacking in joy.

Football Dinosaur

As far as the beautiful game is concerned, you will realise by now, I am very much a traditionalist. That is true in all but one area, I am very much in favour of using technology as much as possible to assist referees in getting the big decisions right.

In every other sport where technology is used it is not only a success, but actually adds to the drama. This is true in particular with rugby and cricket. In our wonderful game, however, many of our people have this toffee-nosed belief that football is somehow removed from all of that. They say that our great game would be ruined as a spectacle if we introduced technology. What a load of baloney!

What is ruining the game for the spectators are the kinds of things I have outlined. We feel frustrated and cheated when good goals are disallowed and vice-versa. If the use of video technology can help get these big decisions right, then it must be trialled at the very least. We need a new breed of administrator, who will not be afraid to give these things a fair crack of the whip. The stakes are so high these days; mega money is involved and people's jobs are on the line as never before.

I don't want to get into the debate about whether technology should be used for offside decisions. I would like to suggest something more radical than that. Let's do away with offside

129

altogether. Surely the point of the game is to get the ball into the opposition net. Offside creates a false situation. Let it go and let's just play football and see if the attackers are cute enough to break down the opposition defences.

Lack of discipline by players is another bone of contention of mine. I would make a rule that only the captain can approach and speak to the referee. Let us see an end to the appalling practice of players surrounding officials in a threatening manner. Maybe a captain could be granted up to two requests in a game. If he genuinely feels that his team have received an unjust decision, he could appeal it and the fourth official, who does not seem to have a lot to do anyway, could review it and communicate his decision with the on-field official. Critics complain that this would cause more breaks in play, but is that any worse than it is at the moment with players refusing to get the required distance back for a free kick? Personally, I would say that a direct free kick is just that and I would not allow a wall to form. Just allow the attacking player a free shot, or pass to a colleague as he wishes.

On the matter of the video replay I actually think the delay would add to the excitement and tension of the occasion, just as it does in other sports. Getting the decision right for the benefit of all must be the number one objective.

Describing the Beautiful Game

Recently I listened to an interview on the Aston Villa website with an American football/baseball commentator. While talking about his art and his love for Aston Villa, he happened to say that football (soccer in his language) was a fast-paced sport on which to commentate and as a result it was more like listening to poetry due to its rhythm. I think that is absolutely true and perhaps the reason why I love to listen to commentators who have a great way with words. For this reason, I list below my all-time favourite commentators on the beautiful game, be they from radio or television:

Simon Brotherton

Brian Butler

David Coleman

Maurice Edelston

Mike Ingham

Peter Jones

Brian Moore

John Motson

Alan Parry

Jonathan Pearce

Martin Tyler

Kenneth Wolstenholme

Of all of those truly brilliant commentators, my favourite has to be Peter Jones. I liked him in the same way I appreciated John Arlott, Brian Johnston and Christopher Martin-Jenkins in cricket, Murray Walker in motorsport, Harry Carpenter in boxing, Norris McWhirter in athletics, Bill McLaren in Rugby Union and Eddie Waring in Rugby League.

When Peter spoke, it was like poetry flowing from his lips and to be fair, that was and is true of the other wordsmiths in my list. I really loved Peter's voice though and he commentated on many events, including a number of the disasters in football already spoken about. Tragically, it was while commentating on the annual Oxford-Cambridge Boat Race that he was taken ill and subsequently died.

On hearing of Peter's sad passing, I wrote to the BBC to tell of my deep admiration of the man and his work. To my astonishment, they wrote back and invited me to Peter's funeral service and then back for tea afterwards at Broadcasting House in London. It was a fabulous service and a fitting tribute to the great man with readings from, among others, Jimmy Armfield. Back at Broadcasting House afterwards I had the pleasure of a quick chat with Jimmy and the person who helped me to my sandwiches was none other than Mike Ingham, another fine commentator, now, sadly from a listener's perspective, retired.

Nowadays there are more live football commentaries than ever before so, of necessity, more commentators. As a result, that means more summarisers who, in the main, talk far too much for my liking. I would rather the summariser make the occasional astute observation and let the commentator get on with describing the game. For radio listeners there is nothing more annoying than the commentator and summariser chatting between themselves, while the match is going on.

The aforementioned Jimmy Armfield is, to my mind, one of the very best succinct summarisers. Of the modern set, I particularly like Ray Wilkins and Chris Sutton.

As far as punditory is concerned, I used to love the banter between Richard Keys and Andy Gray, whereas now I have come to enjoy listening to the views of Joey Barton and I never thought I would be putting that in print. Credit where credit is due though. For all of his well-publicised misdemeanours, Joey does get his views across well; his arguments coming across as well thought out and reasonable.

Chapter 15 - Where Now for Me and The Beautiful Game?

An oft misquoted truth taken from the Bible is that money is the root of all evil. The correct translation is that it is the craving for, or the lust for money which is the root of all evil. There is nothing wrong with money itself. In the right hands, money can be used to do a great deal of good in the world.

As far as top flight professional football is concerned though, it is clearly driven by money and to a large extent the Premier League and other top flight leagues around the world are at the mercy of the television companies, who are pouring mega millions of pounds into the sport for the exclusive rights to broadcast games and, in fairness, why shouldn't they? Football and in particular, the Premier League, is so popular universally now that it is even watched in the poorest and most far-off countries. I recently heard a documentary that revealed the Premier League is even shown in the foothills of the Himalayas, with big screens hanging from trees so that whole village populations can come out and watch.

When I was a child it was the Hollywood film stars who were the highest paid performers and maybe some of them still are. World class footballers though now must rival them for that accolade and deservedly so, many would argue, as they are being watched by audiences the world over. In addition, if the television companies were not making money out of these players then they would not invest the money in the first place.

At present, Association Football, particularly the Premier League and the Football League, is enjoying unbridled commercial success with even, what we might call average players being able to command a fortune in terms of wages.

This development in the last 20 years, has to my mind, removed the players from the fans who love and adore them. It's a shame, these mainly working class kids, who have a talent with a ball at their feet, have now become so famous, living in their luxury mansions, driving their fast cars have become so out of touch with the real world. This is not true of all by any means and what often goes unseen is the enormous amount of charity work individual players take up and that clubs as a whole get involved in.

Many players set up their own charities, whilst others support existing good causes. Aston Villa's very own Bulgarian-born former skipper Stiliyan Petrov, of course, has fought his own personal battle against Leukaemia and apart from setting up his own Foundation has also supported other similar charities. Wealthy players are in a privileged position and while some do mess up their lives because they do not know how to handle their wealth and free time, many others are unsung heroes, doing some amazing work.

Likewise, many clubs have charitable partners with whom they work and support with lots of money and fund-raising events. Aston Villa is no exception and I am proud that my club actively supports a local charity, Acorns Hospice, which seeks to support children with life-limiting conditions and their families. I wholeheartedly applaud this work and it is a thrilling example of how money can be used profitably to encourage, inspire and support people in need.

As long as football increases in popularity around the world and television companies continue to pump money in, then footballers will get richer and richer. I just hope that one day the Premier League will be much more open and competitive with more teams having a chance of winning the title and qualifying for the UEFA Champions League.

What Leicester City achieved in winning the Premier League in 2015/16 so handsomely is truly wonderful and amazing. Once again, the values of team spirit, hard work and good old camaraderie have come to the fore, demonstrating to the world what can be achieved with a little bit of wise management. The Foxes have given hope and encouragement to so-called smaller teams the world over. Maybe the heroic exploits of Iceland and Wales in the European Championships of 2016 are due in some way to the example set by Leicester City, for they have displayed the same kind of work ethic, passion and 'over my dead body' attitude.

Below the Premier League, the Championship is a really exciting and demanding league, as everyone involved at Aston Villa has discovered. Season after season it not only produces many great games, but the race for promotion to the Premier League and the fight for survival from relegation becomes increasingly more tense. Even if you do not support any of the teams in that division, it is nevertheless still compulsive viewing and listening.

As for me, in the words of the song they sing from the back of the Holte End where Ian and I have our seats, I am *"Villa Till I Die"*. So much so that I was highly honoured to be selected as one of their flagship supporters to feature in the *Villa Till I Die* promotional video. I still love the club as much as ever and I log on to the www.avfc.co.uk website several times a day to find any snippets of information to feed my insatiable appetite for the club.

Come on you Villa boys!

Epilogue

At school my favourite teacher was Mr Biddle, the reason being that he picked me for the school football team at the age of 12. I recall so vividly, walking down the main school corridor one Friday lunchtime and looking on the noticeboard, as I did every week, to see who had been chosen to represent Hastings Road under-12s the following day. Week after week I would look in the hope that my name would be there. Then the miracle, for that's what it felt like, happened. My eyes became transfixed to the board as I looked down the team selection to read '10 John Flanner'. I could hardly believe what I was reading, but I had been chosen to wear the same number 10 shirt Johnny Dixon wore as he skippered Villa to that memorable FA Cup triumph back in 1957.

I ran the mile or so home that lunchtime as fast as my legs would carry me to tell my Mum the wonderful news. On arriving at the house, I could hardly contain my excitement and almost jumped into her arms as I exclaimed "Mum, I'm in the team!"

Mum expressed some degree of pleasure, but clearly did not understand just how much this meant to me. From that moment on until I left school at the age of 15, Mr Biddle never left me out of the team. He also happened to be the English teacher and from the moment he chose me, English became my favourite subject. Mr Biddle believed in me and I would have run through the proverbial wall for him.

It's amazing how empowering it can be when someone believes in you isn't it? I explore that theme in more detail in my previous book *Bitzaro to Buckingham* if you should fancy another dose of my writing.

I still cherished the dream of becoming a professional footballer, though gradually it did begin to dawn on me that I was not even as good as half of the other lads in the team. Though very skinny (hard to believe now I know!) I could still tackle pretty well and I had a fierce left-foot shot. I was deadly accurate too and I loved coming up from deep when a corner was taken to hit the ball when it was kicked or headed out of the box. I did smash a few screamers into the net and thought to myself "Stan Lynn would have been proud of that one".

While still playing for the school team and realising I was never going to make it as a career, I began to develop an interest in writing about football. This partly came about because I was frustrated by some of the newspaper reports I read about games I had attended. They either did not capture the feel of what the game was like, or they were inaccurate in describing passages of play. Feeling I could do better, I started to write reports on games and felt they were pretty good when compared to some of the national press reports. Subsequently, when I was about 14 and the careers officer came to the school, asking, "What do you want to do when you leave school?" I replied, "I want to be a football reporter."

I remember the careers man looking very pleased at this and saying something like, "Oh that's good, I have never had a reply like that".

He continued, "Well in that case you will need to stay on at school, get further qualifications and go to college at night to specialise in journalism".

My heart sank because within myself I thought I could not do that. I saw myself as not being very clever and, in essence, gave up on my dream. I left school a few months later and started work as an office junior in an architect's office at Fort Dunlop, the iconic home of the

Dunlop Rubber Company where several members of my family worked, including my dad, uncle and my brother; even my wife worked there for a while too.

Well I guess the lesson is, never give up on your dreams. Here I am some 50 or more years later and I am writing the football story that was in my heart all those years ago. I did have the ability, but lacked the confidence and self-belief at the time to do anything about it.

As you come to the close of this book, I honestly do hope it's been a good read and that it has rekindled some memories for you. If so, then you are probably around my sort of age. That being the case, I wonder what unrealised dreams and potential there is still within you?

This is now my third book in just a few years, I have won the Outstanding Achievement Award at the Civil Service Diversity Awards and more recently enjoyed the prestigious honour of receiving an MBE. Having retired (or should that be re-fired?) at the tender age of 67, I am proud to have launched my own business as an inspirational speaker, and am living proof that you are never too old to realise those unfulfilled ambitions.

If by chance you are a younger reader, then these words are even truer. The only limits in your life are the ones you put on yourself. Dream big and don't let anyone steal your dream.

Postscript – It's Not a War!

I once heard someone say, "If you want to make a point, don't pussyfoot around, use a sledgehammer".

Just when I thought I had said all I wanted to say in this book, I found myself being caught up with the 100-year commemoration of the Battle of the Somme. On Friday 1st July 2016 at 7.28am, along with millions of others across the country, I spent two minutes silently crying out to God, asking "why?" I listened to several programmes on the radio, struggling to comprehend how we could lose nearly 20,000 young men in a few minutes on that fateful day.

Listening to many of the diary entries made by those brave young soldiers, one could not help but be moved to tears. These, and countless thousands of others in the two World Wars gave their lives for our freedom. If they could see our world today in its current state, I wonder if they would ask, "Was it all worth it?" Football of course had a poignant part to play in the historic scenes of the First World War, where the soldiers in No-Man's Land called a ceasefire to play the beautiful game on Christmas Day.

Football, in its purest form, is still a beautiful game, but its good name has been besmirched by many over the years. Even in the 2016 European Championships, the irresponsible actions of some again blackened the name of the sport we love.

I cannot help but think once again of the events immediately following the Hillsborough disaster. Liverpool and Everton, the greatest of rivals (I abhor the word bitter in this context), were destined to meet in the FA Cup Final. I am told that the images of that Final, with opposing sets of supporters linking arms and scarves as the Cup Final Hymn *Abide With Me* was sung, brought tears to many eyes and one leading commentator was heard to say, "In Heaven's name, why does it take a national tragedy to bring people together like this?"

On the battlefields of Europe, when those men went out, laying their lives on the line, for you and me, they did not stop and ask, "which football team do you support?" they joined together to defeat a common enemy. Now I am making an impassioned plea that football supporters the world over will join together in our common love for the beautiful game to defeat tribalism and hooliganism.

It is a total affront to me and, in particular to those who gave their lives in wartime for our freedom, that people like me are not free as things stand to take my grandson Oliver, to Villa Park, simply because his only crime is that he supports Manchester United. If he did come along with me, then he would have to sit with his mouth shut. If he should forget and cheer his team, then he could be set upon and even thrown out of the ground. This is a disgrace and it does not happen in any other sport.

Nelson Mandela had a dream that in South Africa there would come a day when all people would be equal and that black or white, each person would have an equal vote. Dr Martin Luther King had a dream that in the USA black and white would one day have equal rights. Now I have a dream and I invite you to join me on the journey that one day we will all be able to go to a football match and sit anywhere we like with anyone we like. Not just that, but that sportsmanship will return on and off the field. I may well be naive, but I want to see a return to the way things used to be when I could turn up at an away match, make friends with people in the pub or café as we chat about our respective teams. At the end of the game we can shake hands, maybe have a hug and say "See you again at our place".

I think it is strange how some games are called 'friendlies' and derided for that. If a match is a friendly, then what are the other games? They must be unfriendly I guess. Much better I think if we call them practice games and tournament matches. Derbies are certainly not friendly games, these are often the most competitive and lead to the most acts of hooliganism and violence. Kick off times have to be changed on the advice of police as there needs to be more security.

Back in the day, as stated earlier in this book, I loved Aston Villa's derby matches against Birmingham City, West Bromwich Albion and Wolverhampton Wanderers. The atmosphere was incredibly brilliant and spine-tingling. Supporters of each club stood or sat side by side, families stood together as we waved our scarves and chanted for our teams. This was how I came to fall in love with the beautiful game.

I want it back. I say it again, football is not a war, it is a sport; a game to be cherished and respected; a game for all the family.

If Nelson Mandela can hold on to a dream for over 25 years in spite of much personal abuse, to see a nation transformed, then surely we as a peace-loving, world-wide band of supporters of the beautiful game can see things change for the better. As a generation, we owe it to our children and grandchildren to make our football grounds hospitable and welcoming. Just as the guys did at the Battle of the Somme, let us link together in heart and soul, unite as football supporters the world over, for the good of 'The Beautiful Game'.

The legendary Bill Shankly, great though he was, was wrong when he said "Football is not a matter of life and death; it is more important than that".

I am sure he said it tongue-in-cheek with his usual wry smile, but sadly some do make the game more important than life or death. The fact is that it IS a game. Passionate and exciting yes, stirring up deep emotions, but at the end of the day, it is still a game, a sport and not a war. As football supporters, we are a world-wide family of friends and yes, that does mean Aston Villa and Birmingham City supporters, Manchester United and Liverpool supporters, Rangers and Celtic supporters, Real Madrid and Barcelona supporters and so on. Get the message folk, it's more about love than war. Let us embrace one another in the love of the beautiful game.

One final request from me and this is going to be hard also. Can we try and stop using the word 'fans' when referring to football supporters?

As a kid growing up I hardly ever heard the word fan. I was a supporter of Aston Villa and proud to be so, as I am today. Fans, as I understand it are used either for cooling things down, so you could say, cold comfort. Alternatively, they blow out a lot of warm air and hot things up. I hear a lot of that sort of stuff now, especially when clubs are going through tough times. Fans can also be short for fanatics and there are plenty of those around. I much prefer the word supporter, because it is far more positive. When I am going through a difficult time in my life, I need those around me who will give me support and not a kick in the teeth.

When teams or individual players are going through a period of loss of form, the last thing they need are people who get on their backs and start verbally abusing them. That only creates fear and spreads a whole lot of negativity. It is great to have support when things are going well, but it is in times of trouble that players and teams need supporters to get behind them, chant words of encouragement and help the team through a tough spell. That extra bit of support on a 'bad day at the office' can make all the difference and possibly turn a potential defeat into a draw, or a draw into a victory.

I am happy, therefore, to say I am not an Aston Villa fan. But I am most definitely an Aston Villa supporter.

Acknowledgements

I wish to offer my sincere thanks to the following people for their support over the years and in helping me realise my dream in writing this book and getting it published:

Elizabeth Webb for your constant encouragement and belief in me.

Rachel Edwards for patiently editing and proof-reading.

Dave Edwards for cover design and art work.

Mick Tilt for allowing me to use your photographs.

John Lerwill for your valuable insight and comment.

Rob Bishop for your friendship and professional input.

Tony Yorke for helping to pull this project together in the final hours.

My brother Paul and sisters Joan and Susan, who all took turns in keeping my Aston Villa scrapbooks up to date after I went blind. Paul also commentated for me before he too, lost his sight. (Thanks bro!)

Brian Atwick, Ronnie Bowden, Brian Davis, John Place and Richard Akers, all of whom have commentated for me over the years.

Allan Davis and Clive Burbage, Wolverhampton Wanderers supporters and faithful friends from Renewal who share my love of the beautiful game.

Frank Flanner, my late father, for introducing me to Aston Villa in the first place.

Marjorie Flanner, my late mother, for graciously putting up with our moods when we came back from Villa Park after a defeat.

Sylvia Flanner, my beloved wife of 47 years, for allowing me to indulge my passion for the Villa.

Beverley, Sara and Allison, my daughters, for patiently bearing with me in the times I left them to go to Villa Park.

Ian, my son, for the many hours we have spent together at Villa Park and other grounds across the country, for sharing the heartaches of defeat and occasionally the joy of victory. Just like my Dad and I, we have some incredible memories of shared times as father and son supporting our beloved Aston Villa.

John Flanner MBE

www.johnflanner.co.uk

Email: john@flanner.co.uk

Fear Fun and Faith

John Flanner was a typical football-mad teenager until he was robbed of his sight at the age of 19 to a rare hereditary condition. As a shy, self-deprecating young man growing up in 1960's Birmingham, John was already battling many fears and phobias before his subsequent blindness plunged him into a world of darkness.

However, John's determination to succeed, faith in God and the ability to see the potential in every situation led to the rise of a Brummie who conquered his fears and the business world with it. John was the first recipient of the prestigious National Civil Service Diversity Award in 2006 and is now a sought after motivational speaker using his personal experiences in overcoming unexpected disability to inspire and encourage businessmen and women across the UK.

Fear Fun and Faith is the inspirational story of an ordinary man who has led an extraordinary life. Join John as he takes you through the twists and turns of his personal journey with his trademark humour and witty writing style, peppered with plenty of emotional anecdotes and more than one miracle along the way.

***

Fear Fun and Faith is available in all good book stores

ISBN 978-0-9934175-0-4

Bitzaro to Buckingham

Acclaimed writer John Flanner MBE is back with the second instalment of his autobiography that takes us from Bitzaro Palace on the Greek shores all the way back to Buckingham Palace on home soil. Starting with a series of traumatic events on holiday resulting in air ambulance ride back to England, John's story unfolds as he finds himself caring for his wife while facing new challenges in his working career.

The events on that fateful holiday and John's unswerving faith and fervour both personally and professionally, led to him receiving one of the highest accolades, an honour from Her Majesty the Queen. Displaying his heart and his humour in the pages, John's wonderful writing style captivates the reader who will likely experience and equal measure of laughter and tears as he takes them on a journey through the last ten years of his life.

Bitzaro to Buckingham details John's journey from retirement to refirement as he chronicles the launch of his full-time career as a motivational speaker whilst caring for his beloved wife, Sylvia. CEO's and stay at home mothers alike will relate to John's personable character as they read this inspirational story of how one man has defied the odds and continues to reach new heights as he follows God's path for his life.

***

Bitzaro to Buckingham is available in all good book stores

ISBN 978-0-9934175-2-8